"Through remarkable photographs and rich historical insight, this book preserves the memory of Hog Island and its people, capturing a chapter of Eastern Shore history that might otherwise have faded from view. For anyone who cares about coastal heritage, environmental change, or the enduring resilience of island communities, these pages offer both discovery and remembrance."

-Sally Dickinson
Executive Director
Barrier Islands Center

"Curtis and Lynn Badger have a knack for identifying good stories and telling them well. Their ***Broadwater Island: Another Time, Another Place*** is at once an example of how the coming of the railroad to the Eastern Shore of Virginia in the late nineteenth century encouraged Northern investment on the peninsula, the history of a short-lived seaside resort on Hog Island, and the story of a little girl growing up in what she regarded as paradise. The Badgers lavishly illustrate the book with remarkable photographs of island life only recently made available."

- Brooks Miles Barnes
Historian and Author

Broadwater Island

Another Time, Another Place

ISBN 978-1-62806-488-9 (print | paperback)
ISBN 978-1-62806-489-6 (print | hardback)

Library of Congress Control Number 2026908152

Published by Salt Water Media
29 Broad Street, Suite 104
Berlin, MD 21811
www.saltwatermedia.com

On the cover: A group of young men gather at the harbor of Hog Island. In the distance is the oyster house and the fleet of schooners used in the oyster fishery. The picture was taken around 1890, when only a few people were full time residents.

Cover photograph and interior photographs courtesy of the Museum of Northern Arizona, except where noted. Other contributors are cited in the Acknowledgements.

Broadwater Island

Another Time, Another Place

Curtis J. Badger and Lynn M. Badger

This project was made possible
through the cooperation of
the Museum of Northern Arizona in Flagstaff
and the Eastern Shore of Virginia Barrier Islands Center in Machipongo.

Thank you.

Contents

All That Remains 1

The Pictures 3

Joseph Ferrell and Broadwater Island 10

The Pennsylvania Connection 20

The Landscape 29

The Hog Islanders 42

Mr. Cleveland Comes Calling 46

Ivy League Football Comes to Broadwater 54

The Life-Saving Station and the Wreck of the *San Albano* 57

Mary-Russell's Broadwater Island 61

Paradise Lost 66

The Storm of '33 72

The Exodus 76

Coda 79

Acknowledgements 83

Index 85

All That Remains

The landscape you will see here is covered by the ocean today. It is buried beneath the Atlantic, east of the chain of barrier islands that line the Virginia coast. But in another time, it was another place. A century ago, before the sea rose, people lived here and worked here. It was a place of dreams. The dream was called Broadwater, and it belonged to a man from Germantown, Pennsylvania, named Joseph L. Ferrell.

Joe Ferrell was an engineer who worked for the railroad, laying track in a virgin landscape that had known only the footfall of man and beast. Ferrell worked for the Pennsylvania Railroad, and it was his job to design a steel road to run down the narrow peninsula of Virginia's Eastern Shore, a slim spine of land separating the Atlantic Ocean and the Chesapeake Bay. The track would snake its way through forest and farm fields, skirting creeks and bays, until finally coming to an uncelebrated end in a marshy area south of Cherrystone Landing. From there, the railroad would be connected by barges to the port of Norfolk and points south, thus giving the railroad a viable north-south route. The Eastern Shore was the final link in the chain that would revolutionize trade and travel along the east coast.

As Ferrell explored the Eastern Shore, he visited the barrier islands and one in particular caught his eye. Hog Island lay to the north of the island owned by the Cobb family and south of one owned for generations by the Parramores. Hog Island was one of the largest of the chain of thirteen barrier islands that run for more than 100 miles along the Virginia and Maryland coast. It had a wide, sandy beach that stretched as far as the eye could see, and an old maritime forest with an understory kept open by grazing cattle and sheep. There were freshwater springs and lagoons, and dunes glistened in the sun like snowy slopes along the foothills of a mountain range.

A few people had homes on Hog Island. A family named Doughty worked for the government and ran the lighthouse in the dunes on the southern end, and there was a life-saving station that opened in 1875 with a crew that varied from ten or so in the busy winter season to a handful in summer. Other islanders lived in cabins scattered around the upland. They herded their animals, tended their garden, and took what nature provided them. The gathering place was the boat dock and oyster house that lay along the creek on the west side of the island, not far from the lighthouse.

It occurred to Ferrell that once his job was done, the steel road linking the industrial north with the agricultural south, this rural area was going to grow and prosper. The wide beaches on Hog Island were unlike anything up north. The Cobb family operated a rustic hotel on their island south of Hog, and it had a following, even though it was far inferior when it came to high land for building. When he returned to his home in Germantown, he and his wife Elise talked about it. Land was available on the island and they could buy it cheaply. They had family members willing to back them. Joe and Elise had been married less than a year, and this could be the chance of a lifetime. Joe was 44-years old and tired of surveying land for the railroad company. Elise was 26. They were ready to invest in land, make some serious money, and begin raising a family.

This is the story of Broadwater Island, a dream of one man that burned quickly and burned bright, and after more than a century it still warms our past with an unlikely glow. A president spent time on Broadwater. The University of Pennsylvania football team had summer practice there. And a little girl who spent her childhood on the island grew up to be one of the most noted artists in the American Southwest.

And today all of it is gone. The landscape those people inhabited lies beneath the sea, so there are no monuments to explore, no highway markers to celebrate our past. But what we do have are stories passed down, newspaper accounts of the lives of famous men and women. And we have pictures, a great treasure of photographs taken in real time, recording the birth and fleeting life of a special place. And those are all that remains.

The Pictures

In the summer of 2021, I was working on the book *Wilderness Regained – The Story of the Virginia Barrier Islands.* Although wild and remote today, the barrier islands once played a colorful and vibrant role in the history of coastal Virginia. The islands are protected today as national wildlife refuges, state natural area preserves, and as The Nature Conservancy's Volgeneau Virginia Coast Reserve. But many years ago, there were villages, hotels, and gunning clubs that contributed to a fascinating human presence.

In doing research, I discovered that the Museum of Northern Arizona in Flagstaff had a substantial collection of photographs from Hog Island. I was researching the family of Joseph L. Ferrell, an engineer from Pennsylvania who did track design for the railroad when it was being built on the Eastern Shore in 1884. Ferrell and his wife, Elise, bought extensive tracts of land on Hog Island in the late 1880s and created a corporation, Broadwater Land and Improvement Company, to sell lots and build a clubhouse.

The Ferrells promoted their land as Broadwater Island, and they built a cottage and had others built for friends and clients. They moved to the island with their young daughter, Mary-Russell, who spent much of her childhood there. In doing research on the family, I found that Mary-Russell would grow up to become a noted artist in the American Southwest, and that she and her husband co-founded the Museum of Northern Arizona to recognize and promote the artistry of the Native American tribes of that region. I found a biography of Mary-Russell written by Richard and Sherry Mangum titled *One Woman's West – The Life of Mary-Russell Ferrell Colton,* which was published in 1997. The bio included information about Mary-Russell's days on Broadwater Island and the effect the experience had on her life. Mary-Russell died in 1971 from complications of Alzheimers, and the bio said that at the end of her life Mary-Russell still remembered her time at Broadwater, and referred to it as her "childhood paradise."

On a whim, I picked up the phone one day in August 2021 and called the museum and asked to speak with someone in their collections department. I explained that I was researching the early years of the life of the museum's co-founder and asked whether they might have artifacts of any sort. The response was not unexpectedly negative, but I was told I would be notified if anything could be found. To my surprise, a few days later I received a call and was told that the museum had "two files" on Broadwater Island. On August 20 I got an email from their archivist, informing me that the "two files" were in fact photo albums from Broadwater. The museum offered to make photocopies

This photo album held about 35 images from Broadwater Island, as well as a few from the Ferrell home in Pennsylvania.

Scenes on Broadwater Island
My Childhood Paradise
M.R.F.C

Mary-Russell later in life wrote captions in the album and referred to the island as her "Childhood Paradise."

of the albums for me, but the images could not be reproduced. They were for information purposes only.

They sent a total of about 70 images, 35 from each album. I shared the photos with Sally Dickinson, executive director of the Barrier Islands Center, where I served on the board of directors. We were both delighted to find pictures from Hog Island taken from roughly 1888 to 1890. These were family photo albums, with a few pictures taken at the Ferrell family home in Germantown, Pennsylvania. There were family pictures, pictures of cottages Ferrell built, pictures of the lighthouse keeper's family, the life-saving station, and many landscapes. It was a wonderful find, but the mission of the Barrier Islands Center is to find items and share them with the community we serve. And we couldn't share until we had good quality, publishable scans, and permission to use them. And this is where, for multiple reasons, we hit a wall.

Covid was taking its toll and I think the museum was suffering from lack of visitors and programming, their main sources of income. They saw their photo collection as a possible source of funds, but they had strict limitations on their use, and it was very difficult to communicate with them. Sometimes months would pass before I would receive a reply, contact persons would change, and it was very frustrating to realize that these wonderful photographs existed, but we were unable to acquire scans and thus share them with our community.

Things changed in February 2024 when I began dealing with Mary Kershaw, the executive director and CEO. I filled out a form asking for blanket use of all photographs for educational purposes, with credit going to the museum as the source. Two copies of any publication using the photos would be sent to the museum. In early 2025 I began corresponding with Lily Elbaum, their new archivist, and I felt that the museum finally

This map of the Eastern Shore from 1745 referred to the islands and creeks of the seaside in various spellings of the Native term Machipongo.

realized how important these images are to the mission of the Barrier Islands Center and the people of the Eastern Shore of Virginia. You don't often come across photos taken nearly a century-and-a-half ago of a community that today is under the sea.

Lily agreed to make scans of all the images and give us permission to use them, providing we credit the museum as the source. We agreed to pay a suitable fee to compensate the museum for staff time associated with making the scans. In May 2025 we received scans of more than 200 images made from the two Ferrell family albums, plus a third album we had not known about made in 1892-93 by a well-known professional photographer named William Jennings, who worked for the Pennsylvania Railroad.

Jennings's photos were used to promote the Ferrell's Broadwater Island development and were taken as part of a major promotional effort to launch land sales on the island. The Ferrell's second "cottage," designed by the famous architect Theophilus P. Chandler, had been completed in the spring of 1892. In November, the president-elect, Grover Cleveland, would be coming to the island for an extended stay before taking office. Broadwater Island would be in newspapers from coast to coast. It was the perfect opportunity to promote the development.

In all, the collection has about 100 individual images. The museum made multiple scans of some images. Captions and IDs were written in the margins of some photos, and the person scanning made one image to include the caption, and a tighter image just of the picture.

This picture of the "old wharf" shows a double-masted schooner moored near the oyster house. The steam launch Sunshine *is docked to the right of the schooner.*

What the Images Tell Us About Hog Island

One of the most transitional events to have happened on Virginia's Eastern Shore was the opening of the railroad in 1884. Almost overnight, it connected the industrial north with the agricultural south, and on the Eastern Shore it created a great migration, as travel and commerce gradually moved from the wharfs and waterways of the seaside and bayside to the central ridge of the peninsula where new railroad towns quickly grew.

The wonderful thing about the Hog Island photos is that they capture a moment in time that occurred before the existence of the railroad. The railroad brought changes to Hog Island just as it did to every community on the Eastern Shore. In 1884 Hog Island had only a few families as permanent residents, but in twenty years the population would grow as the demand for seafood in northern markets prompted enterprising fishermen to move to the island. A map made in 1851 shows six houses on the island. But the federal census of 1910 showed a population of 173. So, these pictures are like a time capsule, capturing an era that had long disappeared.

Hog Island appears to have been a wild landscape in the late 1880s, remote, untrammeled, and beautiful. The old growth maritime forests had a clear understory kept open by livestock grazing on greenbrier, small shrubs, and grasses. The island had massive dunes, freshwater wetlands, marsh meadows, orchards of fig trees, and a few very modest houses scattered here and there. There was no evidence of a village or community of any sort. The harbor had a boat dock and an oyster house, but very little infrastructure. Schooners and skiffs were moored along creeks that ran through the marsh.

Broadwater, at the time these photos were taken, was not a village, but a term used generically to describe the wide expanse of water that separates the southern barrier islands of Northampton County from the mainland. On old maps, the term broadwater could be found anywhere from the south of Cobbs Island northward to Hog Island and Parramore. It was a description; not a specific place name.

But Ferrell, when working up a marketing plan for his island development, decided that the name Broadwater would be much more appealing and marketable than Hog. The president-elect was coming for a visit, and newspaper headlines announcing that Grover Cleveland was vacationing on Hog Island might conjure an unfortunate image, considering Mr. Cleveland's ample girth. The political cartoonists of the day would no doubt have fun with that.

Census evidence indicates that the population of Hog Island increased after the railroad opened and the market for local seafood grew among east coast cities served by the railroad. According to Charles Sterling's 1903 booklet, *Hog Island Virginia,* thirty-two registered voters lived on Hog Island when Grover Cleveland ran for president in 1892. All of them voted for Cleveland, he wrote.

Hog Island was very much a railroad community, like many towns on the mainland of the Eastern Shore located along the rail line. Hog Island was not on the rail line, but it was connected to it via a wharf east of the Exmore station. The population of Hog Island grew as the demand for seafood in northern cities increased during the early days of the railroad.

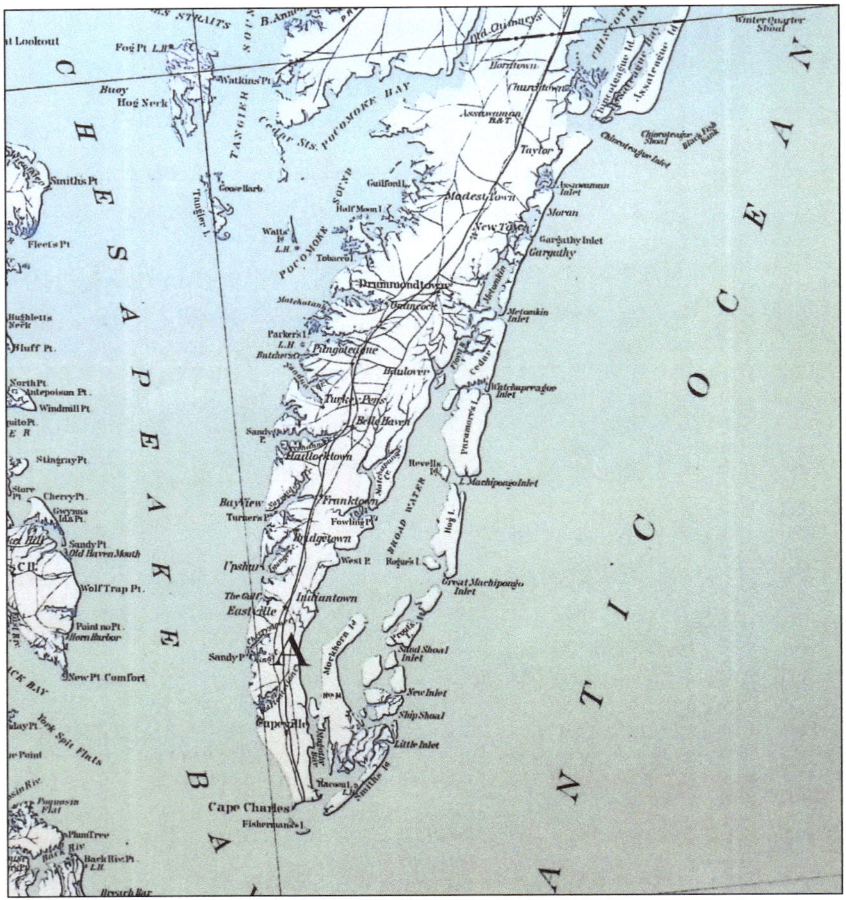

This 1861 Civil War Atlas shows the Broad Water as the bays and tidal flats that separate Parramore, Hog, Cobbs, and Prouts islands from the mainland. Ferrell adopted the term to give to his island development.

Fishing families moved from areas like Long Island Sound and Barnegat Bay southward when those northern areas became fished out, seeking more productive and profitable waters on the Virginia coast. Some of those families, such as the Terrys of Willis Wharf, are still leaders of the seafood industry. The Terrys moved to Virginia from Long Island in 1903, and the fourth generation is involved in the business today, marketing farm-raised clams and oysters nationwide.

Population of Hog Island seems to have peaked around 1910, with the census listing 173 residents, and then it began dropping when the introduction of outboard motors made it unnecessary to live near the fishing grounds. Various publications have stated that Hog Island at one time had a population of 200 to 300 persons, but these totals seem unlikely. I have always pictured a village on Hog Island, sort of an island version of mainland fishing communities such as Oyster or Deep Creek, but I doubt that was the case. There were very few homes during the era when these pictures were taken, but there were obviously more in the decade between 1910 and 1920, when population was at its peak. At that time the island had a small school, a church, and several stores.

Evidence suggests that the Pennsylvania Railroad had a strong interest in the Broadwater Island development. Joe Ferrell worked for the railroad on a contract basis. The photo albums included pictures of railroad officials on the island, and the photographer who produced the third album to market Broadwater

The 1853 Hog Island lighthouse was photographed from the dune side in this picture, giving a good view of the lay of the land in the late 19th century. This was the original lighthouse on Hog Island and was constructed of brick. It was replaced by a metal structure in 1892.

Island was a railroad employee. Pennsylvania Railroad officials were shareholders and investors in both the Broadwater and Parramore Land and Improvement companies, as well as an oyster aquaculture company Ferrell started. As we will see, there was a close relationship between Joe Ferrell's Broadwater Island, the Pennsylvania Railroad, and the University of Pennsylvania.

Joseph Ferrell and Broadwater Island

Broadwater Island was the creation of Joseph Ferrell, but the Pennsylvania Railroad and the University of Pennsylvania were closely involved. Broadwater included a vast network of investors ranging from railroad executives to architects and steel manufacturers, to photographers, book authors, politicians, bankers, and a professional cricket player. All of them had ties to either the railroad or the university.

The Broadwater Island project was emblematic of a wider process described by historian Brooks Miles Barnes in which, during the years following the Civil War, "northern capitalists eyed investment opportunities on the conquered peninsula." Barnes writes in *Steam and Steel – The Eastern Shore of Virginia 1870-1884*, that the Civil War had altered patterns of trade and accelerated profound change, which made the Eastern Shore vulnerable to economic and social pressures from beyond its borders.

The leader of the Broadwater project was Joseph Lybrant Ferrell, who was raised on a farm in Germantown, Pennsylvania, attended Yale University, served as a paymaster in the Union Army during the Civil War, and returned to Philadelphia to start an engineering business. Ferrell married into a prominent family. His wife Elise was from Tennessee and was the daughter of Russell Houston, the chief justice of the Tennessee Supreme Court, who later became president of the Louisville and Nashville Railroad. Her mother's side of the family was descended from James K. Polk, the eleventh president of the United States (1845-49).

Elise Houston and Joseph Ferrell met in Louisville when Ferrell went there at Russell Houston's request to design bridges for the railroad. They were married in 1883 and settled in Philadelphia. When the Pennsylvania Railroad extended its service southward through the Eastern Shore in the early 1880s, Ferrell worked as a contractor, providing engineering services for the new NYP&N Railroad.

While working on the Eastern Shore, Ferrell discovered the barrier islands and realized that the railroad he was helping to build would make these remote, beautiful islands accessible to millions of city dwellers almost overnight.

The railroad opened in 1884, and Joseph and Elise Ferrell went on a buying spree on Hog Island. Between November 25, 1886 and January 4, 1888, they bought three large tracts from William J. Doughty. They also bought various other tracts, mainly on the south end of the island. In November 1889 they purchased more than 500 acres in auctions from the estates of Eli Doughty, Wescoat Churris, and Ann Doughty. By the end of 1889 their holdings on Hog Island had grown to more than 1,500 acres.

The Ferrells clearly had a plan. In 1890 they formed a corporation called the Broadwater Land and Improvement Company and issued stock at $5.00 a share. The corporation had six directors. Ferrell was president, and board members were John C. Sims, Henry Reid, D. S. Newhall, and L. Clarke Davis, all of Philadelphia. George V. Bacon was a resident of St. Paul, Minnesota, formerly of Philadelphia.

The Ferrells transferred their landholdings to the corporation, with the intention of selling residential and resort parcels on the island. The Ferrells hired A.T. Mears and Company of Chincoteague to build cottages for their family and for friends and clients from Philadelphia.

Incorporated under the laws of Virginia

Number 21 — Shares 10

Broadwater Land and Improvement Company

INCORPORATED 1890 — AMENDED 1909

This Certifies that ______ is the owner of Ten Shares of the Capital Stock of

BROADWATER LAND AND IMPROVEMENT COMPANY

Transferable only on the Books of the Corporation by the holder hereof in person or by Attorney upon surrender of this Certificate properly endorsed.

In Witness Whereof, the said Corporation has caused this Certificate to be signed by its duly authorized officers and to be sealed with the Seal of the Corporation this ______ day of ______ A.D. ______

TREASURER — PRESIDENT

Shares $5.00 Each.

COMPANY DISSOLVED BY VIRGINIA CORPORATION COMMISSION, NOV. 22, 1921. FINAL DISTRIBUTION OF ASSETS $2.05 PER SHARE HAS BEEN PAID TO HOLDER OF THIS STOCK.

The Broadwater Land and Improvement Company was chartered in 1890, and stock sold for $5 a share.

The Ferrrells' first cottage was a two-story building with single story additions on two sides.

Judging from photographs taken during the period, the cottages were rustic cabins made with materials sourced locally. The Ferrells' cottage was a two-story frame building with single-story additions on two sides. Roofing and siding appear to have been made of cedar shingles, probably milled on site. Cedar logs supported the porch roof, and the nubs of the limbs remained on the logs. These made convenient hooks for hanging everything from coats and hats to water buckets. Decorative railing was made from the limbs of trees.

The Ferrells decided to move to the island on a semi-permanent basis to market the property, and they wanted a home with more creature comforts and one that would impress future clients. In 1890 they commissioned the nationally known architect Theophilus P. Chandler of Philadelphia to design a seaside cottage. Chandler, who had studied architecture in Paris, came up with a design that a *Philadelphia Ledger* reporter described as "...utterly unlike any other cottage ever built for the shelter of temporary residents by the ocean, or, for that matter, anywhere else. In exterior conformation and interior economy it violates every architectural canon, and is, therefore, both picturesque and comfortable."

The Broadwater Architect

When the Ferrells decided to move to the island in 1890 they hired a highly regarded Philadelphia architect to build a custom cottage for them. They wanted a casual, informal home that had distinctive architectural features, something with flowing lines and minimal detail. Theophilus Parsons Chandler designed a graceful building that perfectly fit the landscape of Broadwater Island. The gently curved rooflines echoed the sloping sand dunes nearby, and the naturally finished red cedar siding seemed perfectly at home nestled into the maritime forest.

T. P. Chandler

Chandler was a Boston native who was educated at Harvard and then studied landscape architecture in Paris. He returned to Boston, but moved to Philadelphia in 1872 to work on a new planned community in the city. He married Sophie DuPont of Delaware and designed homes and worked on restoration projects for her family, including what is now the famous Winterthur Museum in Brandywine Valley.

Chandler designed numerous churches in Philadelphia and the surrounding countryside, and he became known as a restoration architect, designing additions to historic structures in the city.

Chandler's original plan for the cottage called for a steeply pitched roof, but it was decided to alter the design, add another section, and make the roof sloping, echoing the nearby sand dunes that were part of the landscape.

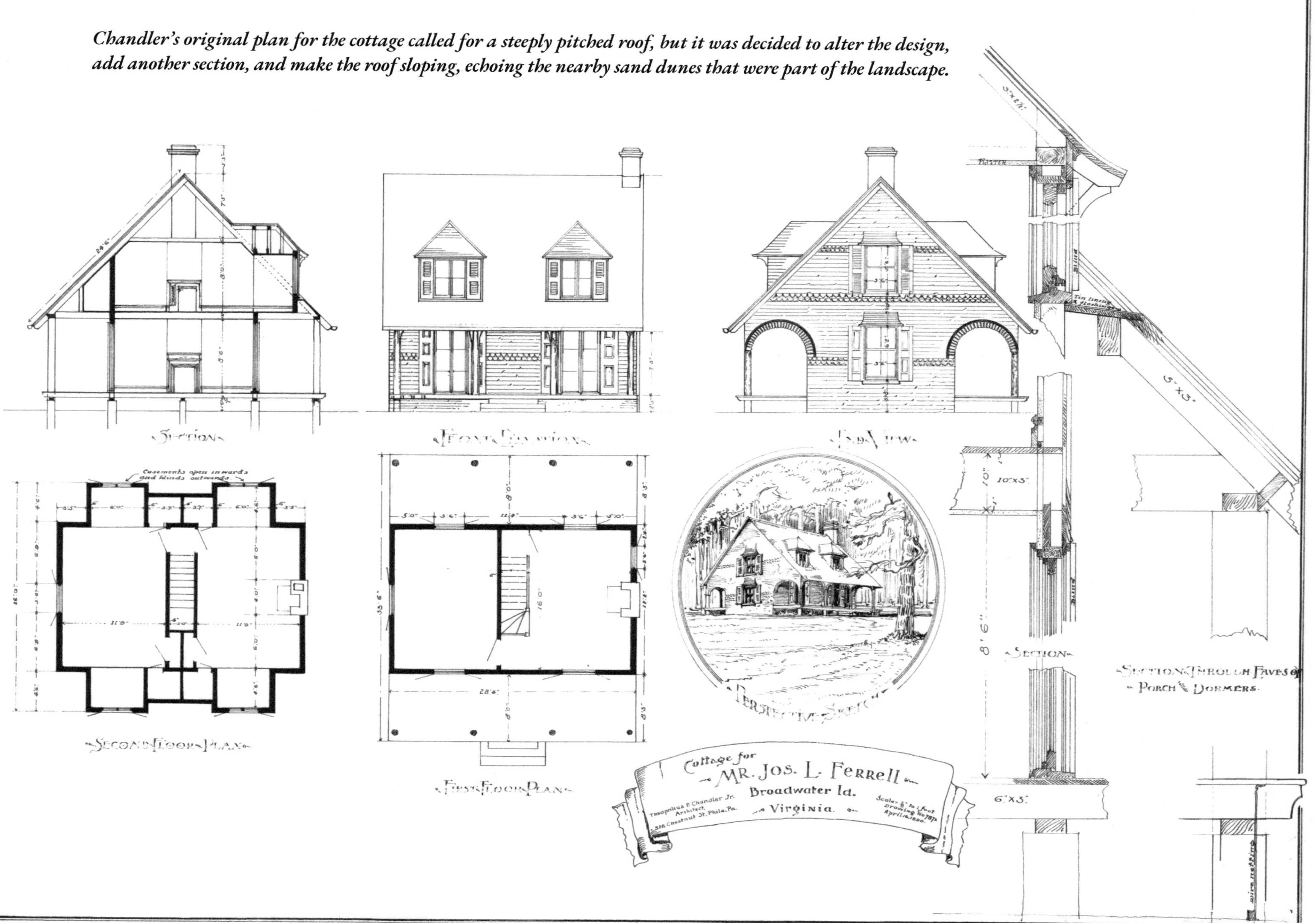

The Ferrell's second cottage, designed by Theophilus Chandler, was an impressive building that fit nicely with the gentle slopes of the island dunes. The Ferrells built their first cottage in 1888 and moved into the larger one designed by Chandler in 1892. A family member took over the original cottage when the Ferrells relocated.

He founded the department of architecture at the University of Pennsylvania in 1890 and became its first head. He and Sophie were very active in the civic and social life of Philadelphia. He died in Philadelphia in 1928 at age 82.

Joseph and Elise Ferrell moved to Hog Island with their daughter, Mary-Russell, and began to actively market property. Early on, Ferrell dropped the name Hog and replaced it with Broadwater, which had been in use as a generic term describing the vast shallow bays, tidal flats, and saltmarsh that separate the southern islands from the mainland Eastern Shore. Ferrell reasoned that Broadwater Island seemed much more euphonious and marketable than the swine reference, and the name caught on among the news media. When a post office opened on the island, it was given the name Broadwater, no doubt at Ferrell's urging.

The Ferrells built a large clubhouse in a pine grove adjacent to their cottage, and memberships were offered to well-off sportsmen, mainly from Philadelphia. The club had approximately fifty members. Waterfowl hunters would come in winter, and family groups would gather on the island year around.

Ferrell was president of the club. Members included executives from the Pennsylvania Railroad and its subsidiaries, lawyers, steel manufacturers, bankers, owners of shipping companies, a shoemaker, a professional cricket player, and a college professor.

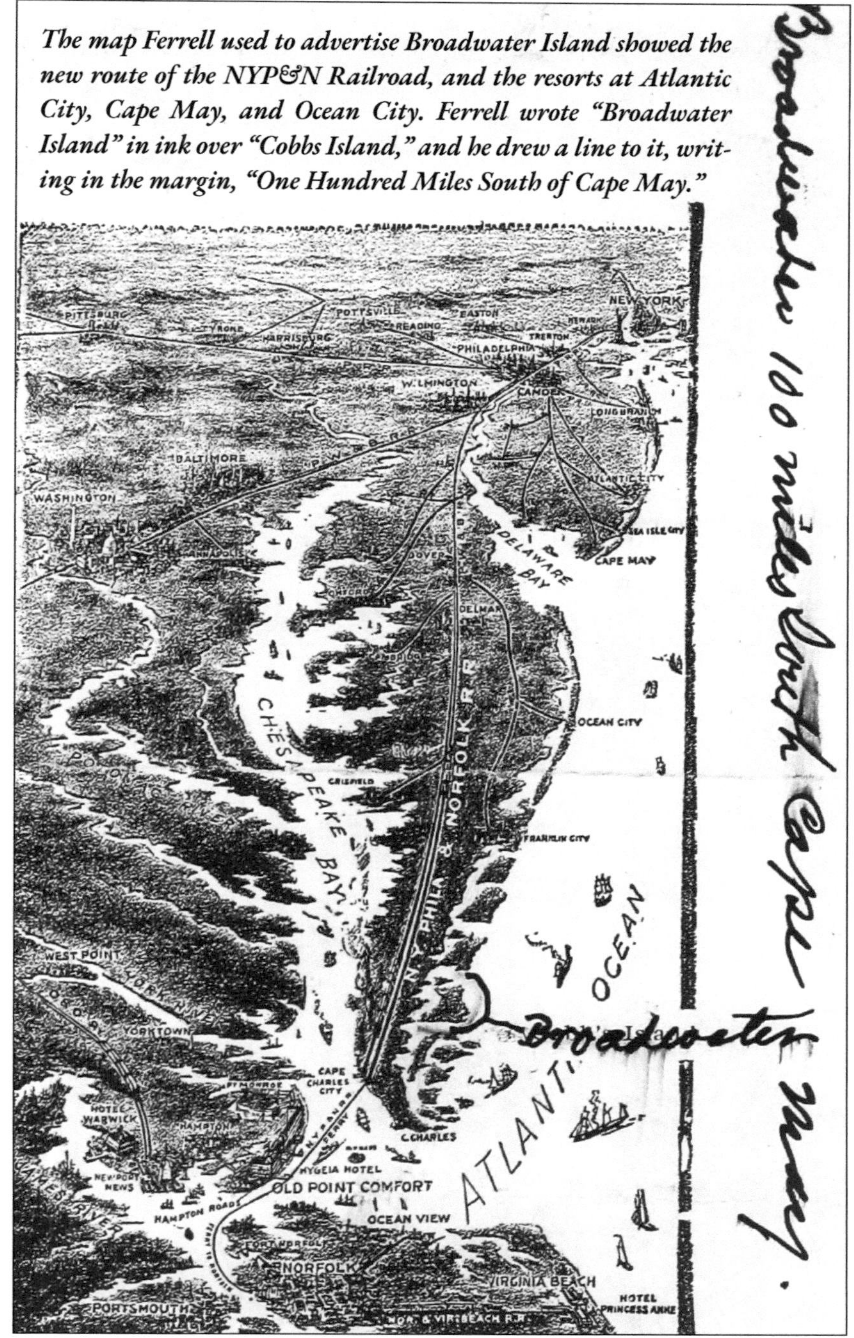

The map Ferrell used to advertise Broadwater Island showed the new route of the NYP&N Railroad, and the resorts at Atlantic City, Cape May, and Ocean City. Ferrell wrote "Broadwater Island" in ink over "Cobbs Island," and he drew a line to it, writing in the margin, "One Hundred Miles South of Cape May."

The Ferrells built a clubhouse near their cottage and offered annual memberships. Most of the members were associated with the railroad or related industries.

The clubhouse was a spacious building that would accommodate about 50 guests.

The porch of the clubhouse.

The clubhouse was located in a wooded area near the Ferrells' cottage.

The reading room of the clubhouse.

Joe Ferrell, seated, has a conversation with a hunter on the island.

Ferrell bought a mainland hummock on Brownsville Farm from Capt. Orris A. Browne, and a small clubhouse was constructed where visitors could await transportation to the island. This clubhouse was used as lodging during the latter days of the Broadwater Club. A hummock is an area of woodland slightly higher in elevation than the surrounding marshland, sort of a wooded island amid a sea of spartina grass.

Ferrell expanded his operation northward, and in February 1892 the Parramore Land and Improvement Company was chartered, with the purpose of constructing residential and resort properties on Parramore Island. The directors named in the charter were Joseph L. Ferrell, president; Henry Whelan, vice president; Theodore Frothingham, treasurer; William McGeorge, Jr.; William M. Levring; William Hacker; and

Joseph S. Smith, all of Philadelphia. Ferrell gave his address as Broadwater Island, Virginia.

Ferrell also incorporated an oyster aquaculture business that operated on Broadwater Island. The Virginia General Assembly in March 1896 chartered the Broadwater Oyster Association, whose purpose was to "promote, by the application of scientific methods, by experimental research, and by all other appropriate means, the propagation, cultivation, and improvement of the oyster."

Directors of the association included three local men – Zoro Willis, O. F. Mears, and G. S. Kendall – and six from Philadelphia. The Philadelphians were Thomas S. Parvin, John C. Sims, Samuel T. Wellman, Frank Hipple, Daniel S. Newhall, and William C. Alderson.

All were successful businessmen. Sims was an executive with the railroad and Wellman owned a steel mill in Philadelphia that supplied rails for PRR. Frank Hipple was president of Real Estate Trust Company, a Philadelphia bank. Daniel Newhall was a former professional cricket player who worked with Sims as assistant secretary of the railroad.

In November 1892 president-elect Grover Cleveland came to Broadwater for nearly two weeks of duck hunting, and Broadwater Island was in newspapers from coast to coast. The Ferrells' second cottage, the one designed by T.P. Chandler, was completed that spring, and the president-elect and his aid, L. Clarke Davis, a friend of the Ferrells, were house guests.

Elise Ferrell poses for the camera while seated on the limb of what appears to be a large wild cherry tree.

Cleveland returned as president the following May for a week of fishing and shorebird shooting, and again Broadwater was in the national media. Ferrell could not have devised a better publicity campaign. Newspaper coverage frequently suggested that the entire island was owned by the Broadwater Club, and this suggestion was not quickly refuted.

The Pennsylvania Connection

As Ferrell established his three separate corporations, along with the Broadwater Club, he looked to Pennsylvania friends for support. His architect, Theophilus P. Chandler, founded the department of architecture at the University of Pennsylvania. L. Clarke Davis, the advisor to the president-elect, was the managing editor of the *Philadelphia Ledger.* The photographer who took the promotional pictures to market Broadwater Island, William Jennings, was an employee of the Pennsylvania Railroad and was known as the first to successfully photograph lightning. He also was the first to make aerial photographs of the Philadelphia skyline from an untethered balloon.

The Broadwater Club did not consist of a group of good-old-boy duck hunters getting together for a weekend of poker and beer. Most members were owners of corporations, bankers, politicians, and high-ranking officials in the Pennsylvania Railroad.

The Bayard family of Delaware, one of the original cottage owners on the island, produced four members of the United States Senate. Thomas F. Bayard, who died in 1898, was a contemporary and friend of Grover Cleveland. In the Democratic national convention of 1884, he finished second to Cleveland for the presidential nomination. After the election, Cleveland named him Secretary of State. In Cleveland's second term, he named Bayard as America's first ambassador to Great Britain. When Cleveland visited Broadwater Island in 1892, he likely called on Bayard at his cottage.

The *Lancaster Intelligencer,* in a story on Bayard's passing, said "he did more, perhaps, to lay the foundation for a revival of good fellowship between England and the United States than any other one man."

One of the more active promoters of Broadwater Island was John Clark Sims, executive secretary of the Pennsylvania Railroad, whose family was prominent among the business and social elite of Philadelphia. Sims arranged to have the University of Pennsylvania football team hold summer practice on Broadwater Island in 1894, giving the island national media attention for two months.

Sims was a Philadelphia native, born in 1845, who graduated from the department of art at the University of Pennsylvania in 1865. He then studied law and was admitted to the Philadelphia bar in 1868. He joined the railroad as assistant secretary in 1876, and five years later was promoted to secretary. He also was secretary of several smaller rail lines under PRR ownership.

According to his obituary in the January 7, 1901 *Altoona Tribune,* "Mr. Sims's position placed him in the closest confidential relations with the officers and board of directors, and his

The Bayard family of Wilmington, Delaware was one of the first to occupy a cottage on Broadwater Island. This is the James Bayard family. The Bayards had four members who served in the United States Senate. Thomas Bayard was a contemporary of Grover Cleveland, who finished second to Cleveland in the 1884 Presidential Primary. Cleveland named him Secretary of State during his first term, and Ambassador to Great Britain during his second.

The Bayards' cottage, like others on the island, was built with wood milled on-site. Shingles were made from local eastern red cedar trees, and the limbs of pine trees were used for trim and decorative touches.

responsibilities were of the gravest character. He married Grace L. Patterson, a sister of C. Stuart Patterson, president of the Commercial Trust Company, of this city, and a director of the Pennsylvania Railroad. He is survived by her and five children."

The University of Pennsylvania Archive Center has a lengthy biography of Sims, who was active in university matters throughout his life:

"Sims's interest in the university did not flag after his graduation. He was greatly involved in Penn athletics as president of the University of Pennsylvania Athletic Association and of the Pennsylvania Railroad Athletic Association. He became instrumental in cricket matters while serving on the committees managing some of the most important international matches of the day. He served as a trustee of the University from 1885 until his death on January 6, 1901. At the time of his death he represented the trustees of the university on the faculty committee on athletics."

Sims died at the relatively young age of 55. He was hospitalized for appendicitis, was operated on successfully, but died of heart failure while in the hospital recovering from the surgery.

Samuel T. Wellman (1847-1919) was a Philadelphia industrialist and inventor of the iron blast furnace, whose steel mill in Philadelphia employed 1200 workers who produced track for the railroad. Wellman was a member of the Broadwater Club and served as a director of the Broadwater Oyster Association.

Another director was Daniel S. Newhall (1849-1913) a Penn grad and a professional cricketer who played for the Philadelphia cricket team. He and John Sims were teammates when they were students at Penn and remained close throughout their lives, largely through a shared interest in athletics, and cricket in particular. Newhall was a director of both Broadwater Land and Improvement and the Broadwater Oyster Association.

William Hacker, a director of the Parramore Land and Improvement Company, was another member with a railroad background. Hacker was auditor of the Canal and Coal divisions of the Pennsylvania Railroad, and he also served as a director of the Provident Life and Trust Company and of the National Bank of the Republic. He served as treasurer of the Zoological Society of Pennsylvania.

Joseph S. Smith, also a director of the Parramore company, was a shoemaker. His family founded the M.A. Smith Company, a prominent manufacturer of shoes in Philadelphia, a city famous for shoemaking since colonial times.

William D. Windsor was in the transportation industry, but his interest was in sea-going commerce. He was a director of the Boston and Philadelphia Steamship Line.

Sydney G. Fisher was the author of the book *The Making of Pennsylvania* and was on the faculty of the University of Pennsylvania. Fisher was a club member.

It was the 1892 visit of Grover Cleveland that put Broadwater on the map, both literally and figuratively. The president-elect spent twelve days on the island, and the visit was arranged by

The island had many osprey nests. This one near the clubhouse appears to have a bird on the nest.

This is the rear view of the clubhouse, which one newspaper described as a "commodious" structure. The clubhouse faced a pine forest on one side and the other was situated on the edge of a grassy meadow where cattle and sheep grazed.

L. Clarke Davis, the newspaper executive, along with Ferrell, Sims, the Bayards, and other club members and directors. Davis used the president-elect's visit to publicize the island in newspapers, dealing directly with the news media and writing some reports himself.

The *Tyrone Daily Herald* of Tyrone, Pennsylvania published this story on the Broadwater Club in its November 25, 1892 edition. The president-elect was on Broadwater Island at the time. The story lists some prominent Philadelphians who were members and investors in Broadwater.

Broadwater, formerly known as Hog Island, is one of the most romantic spots on the Atlantic coast and is equally famous for its hunting and fishing. A small private club composed principally of well-known Philadelphia gentlemen here own or control the greater part of it and erected hereon an attractive and comfortable clubhouse, of which they and their families make almost constant use. The clubhouse, a commodious frame structure, capable of accommodating from 40 to 50 persons, is situated on an elevation commanding an excellent view of the sand hills, the broadwater, the lighthouse, and the life-saving station on the island and it is surrounded by majestic pines.

It is the sportsman's paradise and the immense flocks of redheads, teal, mallards, and wild goose on the broadwater have

The Bayards had a large family that spent summers on Broadwater to escape the heat of the city. A handwritten note in the margin of one of the Bayard photos, said that the Bayards "were friends of Mother's."

John Clark Sims, executive secretary of the Pennsylvania Railroad, was an investor in the Broadwater project who arranged to have the Penn football team have summer practice on the island in 1894. Sims and his wife had five children, and the family spent a lot of time on Broadwater Island. Sims was a Philadelphia native who graduated from the department of art at the University of Pennsylvania in 1865. He then studied law and was admitted to the Philadelphia bar in 1868.

L. Clarke Davis, pictured with his two sons on the clubhouse grounds.

Clarke Davis was a member of a literary family. He was a journalist, his wife, Rebecca Harding Davis, was a well-known novelist, and their two sons would grow up to have literary careers of their own.

gained for it the reputation of being the finest ducking grounds along the eastern coast. As a fishing resort it is equally famous. The excellence of its oysters are also acknowledged. The waters are teeming with drumfish which when large weigh from forty to fifty pounds. James P. Bayard also resides on the island.

Among the well-known members of the club are Judge Henry Reed; Henry la Barre Jayne; James Bayard; Theodore Frothingham; L. Clarke Davis; J. C. Sims, Secretary, and D. S. Newhall, assistant secretary of the PRR; Frank K. Hipple; Clement Biddle; William D. Windsor of the Windsor Line; Sydney G. Fisher; Clement A. Griscomb, president of the International Navigation Company; William Hacker, auditor Canal and Coal Companies of the Pennsylvania Company; George C. Thomas of Drexel and Co.; John Lowher Welsh; James Rawle; Joseph C. Fraley; William A. Patton, vice president, and H. W. Dunne, superintendent of the New York, Philadelphia, and Norfolk Railroad; Dr. John Marshall, dean of the Medical Department of the University of Pennsylvania; Thomas S. Parvin; Frederick W. Morris; and Henry L. Davis.

The five Sims children and their dog on the woodland road.

The Landscape

The wonderful thing about the Broadwater photographs is that they capture a landscape previously experienced only by the spoken word, or through memoirs passed along from one generation to the next. Place-names tended to be a combination of careful observation and imagination.

Rum Hill, for example, was a large sand dune on the island rumored to have been a hiding place where pirates stashed their loot, including the occasional cask of rum. Rum Hill is photographed and identified, although no rum is evident.

Cherry Ridge was a stretch of highland on the island where a few trees (cherry?) are scattered across a meadow of grassland where cattle and sheep are photographed as they graze.

The name Burn Hill had an obvious source, judging from the scorched grasses along the dunes. Across Levels also had very literal roots. The photo was taken from a high point with a gnarled pine tree framing the landscape below, which appears to be a very flat salt-pan, possibly caused by overwash during high tides.

Fig Orchard, in a photograph by William Jennings, is a grassy meadow with a split-rail fence and a small cottage in the background. Fig trees are planted along the fence line. Hog Island had its own cultivar of fig, which is still being propagated today.

Burn Hill

Cherry Ridge

Across Levels

Fig Orchard

The Old Fig Orchard.

First lighthouse on Hog Island

Osprey Grove

Osprey Grove was a wooded area where ospreys nested. Ospreys were plentiful on Hog Island, often nesting in dead pine trees. Most landscape photos of the island during this era had numerous osprey nests visible in the distance. Better known as fish hawks on Hog Island, ospreys found the shallow bays and creeks around the island a good source of food. The original Hog Island lighthouse had been abandoned when this photo was taken in the early 1890s. An osprey made itself at home in a pine snag, however.

Marsh with osprey nest

Rum Hill

Rum Hill

And there is Rum Hill, 100 feet high, one of the most conspicuous features of the island. Whether true or not, a curious tale is connected with the hill and its name. It is said that a hundred years or so ago a West Indian rum trader went ashore off Hog Island and was broken up during a violent storm. She was loaded with casks of liquor destined for New Bedford, and the Hog Island wreckers recovered the cargo as it came ashore.

There was no place of storage for the hogsheads and they were piled upon the island, well out of the way of the waves, but, as it transpired, not of the winds. A big storm came up. The light, white sand of the island was blown upon the pile of rum casks until they were concealed, and finally buried deep beneath a cone of salted grains of sand that drifted upon it until the islanders could not remove it. "They" say the rum is still beneath the sand -- that the salt in their covering must have preserved the casks from disintegration. Who knows? Perhaps it is.

At any rate, say the natives, if you don't believe this story, why there's the proof -- there's the hill. "Rum Hill" is as large around at its base as Union Square. So white and sparkling is it in the sunlight that seafarers catch sight of it from a long distance.

From:
Mr. Cleveland's Quaint Old Shooting Resort
New York Herald
New York
December 4, 1892

Woods Road linked several of the cottages, and is photographed with a horse and cart in the distance. The road was cut through what appears to be a forest of old growth pines, evidence of the magnificent coastal forests that once thrived on the barrier islands. Unlike forests today, there is no understory of greenbrier or small saplings. Grazing cattle and sheep make the forest appear park-like.

The Government Road was a modest byway cut through the woods, just wide enough to accommodate a horse and cart, or ox and cart. It was built by the government to transport food, fuel, and other necessities from the boat dock to the lighthouse and life-saving station.

Elise Ferrell with "Grandma Robbins's Cottage" in the background

The caption with this picture read "oak pine," apparently referring to the large tree on the left side of the road.

At left on top: This wooded grove looks as though it had been recently mowed, but grazing livestock such as cattle and sheep keep the undergrowth under control. The animals lived well on natural forage and had plenty of fresh water to drink in natural springs.

At left on bottom: This was Hog Island's means of transport in the late 19th century. Wagons were used to handle loads ranging from lighthouse supplies to fishing and boating equipment.

Elise Ferrell and her sister, Mary-Russell Buchanan

The most spectacular landscape on Hog Island were the massive sand dunes and the wide, hard-packed beach. Elise Ferrell and her sister, Mary-Russell Buchanan, pose for the photographer in the dunes.

The Hog Island dunes looked like this in the late 1800s, but sea level rise coupled with tropical storms took its toll on the dunes over the years.

Mary-Russell Ferrell Colton wrote in a caption with this picture that she used to slide down the dunes when she was a child on Hog Island.

Mary-Russell wrote a caption for this photograph, "The finest beach I have ever seen." This picture is probably of Elise Ferrell holding an infant Mary-Russell in her lap. The photo is a bit soft, but it does appear that she is holding a baby, blurred by movement.

Joseph Ferrell leans against the base of a pine snag in the dunes.

*The caption for this picture read "spirit of pain tree," likely because it had numerous long, sharp briars. The picture is of Joe Ferrell with a visitor, possibly L. Clarke Davis. The tree is likely a Hercules Club tree (*Zanthoxylum clava-herculis*), a native of the coastal plain that favors sandy, well-drained soil. Native Americans and early settlers called the tree the "toothache tree" because chewing on the bark or fruit was said to cause numbness to the gum and tongue.*

The Hog Islanders

Most of Virginia's barrier islands have been populated by transients. People stayed in hotels and gunning clubs, they came to celebrate pony and sheep roundups, they fished or enjoyed a day at the beach, they worked for a while at a life-saving station. And then they left.

But Hog Island was made up of Eastern Shore people. They were residents whose roots went back generations. They were part of us, related if not by blood, then certainly in spirit. My family's roots go back to Red Bank Landing, where my great-grandfather John had a farm and operated a small shipping business. When he looked to the east, he saw Hog Island. When a Hog Islander looked to the west, he saw John's farm. They were the same people, just with different views.

Hog Island, and to a lesser extent Assateague, was not just an island, but a community of people whose lives and families were intertwined. At its peak around 1910, Hog Island was populated by more than 100 people, Assateague by about two dozen.

Ralph T. Whitelaw, in his two-volume history, *Virginia's Eastern Shore*, writes that the island was first patented in 1681 by four men: Thomas Hunt, John Floyd, Edmund Bibby, and George Clark. The patent was for 2,200 acres. In 1687 the four received another patent, this time for a total of 3,350 acres.

At that time the island was referred to as Hogg Island. The Indian name had been Machipongo, and the island also was known as Shooting Beach. In 1688 the island was divided among the patent holders and their heirs. As was the case with most of the islands at the time, it was used primarily to pasture livestock, and this likely accounts for the name. Feral animals lived on Hog Island into the late 1970s, when The Nature Conservancy had a wild west style cattle roundup and removed the remaining animals. National Geographic filmed the event.

In 1752 Thomas Hunt's heirs sold 139 acres to Peter Dowty, Jr., and Whitelaw speculates that this might have been the first transaction on the island for residential purposes. It also introduces a surname that, with a less phonetic spelling, became widely known on Hog Island. Of the forty-two families listed as Hog Island residents in 1903, eight were Doughtys.

The first people to live permanently on Hog Island were likely there to tend the animals, and the formation of a community probably began soon after the American Revolution ended. The formation of a community on Hog Island had many parallels with the one on Assateague. Both were used as pasture, both had a lighthouse and life-saving station, which employed local people, and both were in close proximity to marketing resources – Chincoteague in the case of Assateague, and Willis Wharf, and later Exmore, in the case of Hog.

George Doughty served as lighthouse keeper on Hog Island from 1886 until 1908, making him one of the longest tenured keepers in the service. The position brought with it a wide range of responsibilities. In addition to keeping the light burning, Doughty was the de facto "mayor" of Hog Island. When dignitaries visited the island, it was Doughty who entertained them and showed them around. He guided for president-elect Grover Cleveland when he spent twelve days duck hunting on the island in the winter of 1892. Doughty had quarters at the lighthouse compound, but the family lived in a neat frame house adjacent to a marsh meadow on the island.

Lizzie Phillips was one of the best known residents of the island. Charles Sterling, in his 1903 booklet on Hog Island wrote, "Among the older residents of Hog Island is Mrs. Lizzie Phillips. She owns a large number of cattle, sheep, and hogs, and is often seen standing by the corner of her log cabin calling her stock; and more frequently tramping over the meadows, through mud and water ankle deep, driving her herd homeward." With her is her brother Richard and a boy identified as Ray.

George Doughty was photographed with his wife and their children.

Lizzie's brother Richard relaxes in a marsh meadow. According to the MilesFiles genealogy web site, Lizzie was 27 years old at the time of the 1870 census and was a school teacher. Richard was listed as a fisherman and was ten years older than Lizzie, who was about 47 when this picture was taken.

One thing Hog had that Assateague lacked was fertile soil, making it possible to sustain a much larger community. Indeed, people lived simply but well on both islands. The sea provided a bounty nearly year around. Migrating shorebirds were killed in spring, waterfowl in winter. The eggs of gulls, rails, and other birds were a special treat during spring nesting season. This natural larder supplemented the vegetables people harvested from their gardens, as well as hogs, chickens, and other animals. Written accounts portray Hog Island as a source of the earth's bounty, where watermelons grew so large they were "too big to steal." Hog Island figs were a cultivar all their own, and specialty nurseries still offer these heirloom varieties.

The people who lived on Hog and Assateague shared similar character traits. Some visitors described them as lazy, but a more balanced assessment of life on Hog Island is presented by L. E. Doughty in his 57-page memoir, *A Narrative About Life on Hog Island, Va.*, published in 2002 by Hickory House. Doughty grew up on Hog Island but moved to New Jersey later in life. He depicted life on the island as a life of independence, but a life that centered around working on the water was never easy. Doughty writes about oystering, clamming, fishing, and hunting waterfowl, and he does so in a way that makes these activities not necessarily work, but simply a way of living. It was what one did in order to exist.

The Broadwater photographs document the stark difference between native islanders, whose rhythm of life was tuned to the seasons, the tides, and the whims of nature, and the wealthy and privileged men and women from northern cities.

Mr. Cleveland Comes Calling

President-elect Grover Cleveland arrived on Hog Island on November 23, 1892 and spent nearly two weeks there. He had just been elected to a second term, replacing the incumbent, Benjamin Harrison, who had defeated him four years earlier. This was Cleveland's first trip to Hog Island, but he was familiar with the Eastern Shore of Virginia. He had visited during his first term, in May 1886, spending a night at the Hollywood Farm near Cape Charles City as the guest of Congressman William L. Scott, one of the founders of the New York, Philadelphia and Norfolk Railroad.

The stated reason for the 1892 visit was to provide Mr. Cleveland with a private refuge where he could rest and recover from the election campaign and indulge in one of his favorite winter sports, duck hunting. As soon as the election ended, the president-elect was besieged by backers seeking influential positions in the new administration, and the privacy afforded by an island separated from the mainland by ten miles of open water would provide relief.

Not coincidentally, the visit would also provide the backers and investors in Broadwater Island an unprecedented opportunity to gain national publicity and generate land sales. Mr. Cleveland did not allow interviews with the press, but visiting reporters were given ample opportunity to see the island and to document the president-elect's daily adventures. Broadwater Island was in the national media for two weeks in the fall of 1892, with newspaper coverage ranging from Philadelphia to San Francisco.

The organizers of Mr. Cleveland's visit were all stockholders of the Broadwater Land and Improvement Company and members of the Broadwater Club. L. Clarke Davis, the newspaper publisher and presidential advisor, accompanied Mr. Cleveland on his daily outings, and the two men shared the recently completed T.P. Chandler cottage with the Ferrell family. During the president-elect's stay, Ferrell invited numerous potential investors to visit the island and perhaps get to meet the famous visitor while they toured the island landscape.

The visit was a great public relations success for Ferrell and his investors. Newspapers across the country ran stories daily about Mr. Cleveland's adventures, and by the end of the visit, remote and desolate Hog Island had morphed into Broadwater Island, a private retreat where entry was limited to members exclusively.

The December 3, 1892 edition of Harper's Weekly *featured a full page of photo-illustrations by artist Frank H. Taylor. The bottom illustration shows Rum Hill adjacent to the original lighthouse. The Ferrell cottage designed by Chandler is on the left, and the Broadwater clubhouse is in the trees on the right. Taylor was a prolific lithographer and illustrator who lived in Philadelphia and was known for documenting local landmarks.*

Hot off the Press

Remote as Africa

This story from the *Star-Independent* of Harrisburg, Pennsylvania on November 23, 1892 said the island was as remote as Africa, and that boats were not allowed to land there without permission of the club. At this point the corporation was by far the largest landowner on the island.

An overland trip of ten miles is necessary to reach the coast, and then will come a ten-mile trip by water to Hog Island, or Broadwater Island, as its new owners have named it. Here the president-elect will be about as completely cut off from the outside world as though he were in Africa. The island is the property of the Broadwater Club, an organization composed of about fifty wealthy Philadelphians, and no boats can land thereon unless by permission of the club. The club house is a very comfortable structure, although the island itself is bleak and barren. There are any quantity of game on it, however; in fact, it is a perfect hunters paradise, and Mr. Cleveland, during his two-week stay will probably burn great quantities of powder.

Groves of Pine and Sassafras

The *Republican Herald* of Schuylkill, Pennsylvania in its November 25, 1892 edition gives a nice description of the landscape, including "the groves of pine and sassafras and the orchards of fig trees." The reporter stated that all the local islanders, with the exception of those at the life-saving station, were in the employ of the Broadwater Club. Ferrell was trained as a mechanical engineer, but he enjoyed experimenting in different fields. While on Broadwater he engaged in oyster aquaculture, and in 1894 formed the corporation Broadwater Oyster Association to propagate oysters. Later in life Ferrell would invent a liquid that would fireproof materials, and he spent the last few years of his life promoting it. He likely was employing local residents in the aquaculture venture, as well as in various roles in maintaining the club.

President-elect Cleveland is enjoying himself quietly on Broadwater Island, the beautiful but isolated resort which is owned by the Broadwater Club. It is nineteen miles from Exmore Landing (today Willis Wharf), which place is two miles from Exmore Station on the New York, Philadelphia & Norfolk Railroad. The private steam launch Sunshine *plies between the land and the island over a course which follows Machipongo Creek for five and a half miles. The island is nine miles long and three miles wide, and contains a population of 21 families.*

The president-elect and his friends Charles B. Jefferson and L. Clarke Davis are the guests of Joseph L. Ferrell, president of the club, at his cottage, which stands a short distance from the clubhouse, the latter standing in a grove of pine trees half a mile inland. Mr. Davis is a member of the club.

Although the object of Mr. Cleveland's visit is to secure absolute quiet and much needed rest, he expects to spend some time in duck shooting.

A reporter of the National Press went to the island last evening and presented his card to the president-elect. He was received courteously, but Mr. Cleveland begged to be excused from submitting to an interview. He, however, expressed himself as being delighted with his surroundings, and said that it was his intention to remain on the island for five or six days. Then he will join Mrs. Cleveland in Lakewood, N.J.

It does not seem possible that a more isolated spot could have been selected where Mr. Cleveland might be free from the various annoyances to which he was subjected in New York.

The island's population, with the exception of the crew of the United States Life-saving Station, are in the employ of the club.

One-fourth of Broadwater Island is covered with splendid groves of pines, sassafras, and orchards of fig trees. This portion is a succession of mounds, but the remainder is level and slopes to what is considered the finest beach in America.

Mr. Cleveland Makes an Impression

When your dad is in the business of marketing high end real estate, it gives you the opportunity to meet the rich and famous. The *San Francisco Examiner* ran a story in its December 6, 1892 edition about three teenagers who got to hunt ducks with Mr. Cleveland. The teens included Thomas Newhall, the son of Daniel S. Newhall, a director of the Broadwater corporation, and two of his friends. Thomas grew up to become a prominent banker in Philadelphia.

Grover Cleveland is making a tremendous impression as a sportsman on the minds of Philadelphians who have been shooting with him down on Broadwater Island, says the Philadelphia Press. Three of them returned home yesterday with a hamper full of ducks and a mind full of notions about the big man who has just carried the country. These three are Kane Green, Thomas Newhall, and Howard Chase.

They all live in West Philadelphia. None of them vote as yet, and two of them are students at Haverford College. They are young and impressionable, and therefore all the more susceptible to Mr. Cleveland's prowess with the gun as well as the ballot. They spent their Thanksgiving holidays at Broadwater and shot at ducks from behind blinds adjoining those used by Mr. Cleveland.

They spent some evenings also at the Broadwater clubhouse, which Mr. Cleveland visited. The house is about 150 yards distant from the residence of Mr. Ferrell, where the next president is comfortably domiciled.

"I tell you," said one of them enthusiastically yesterday, "Mr. Cleveland looks every inch a sportsman when clad in his gunning suit of heavy gray cloth, with double-breasted sack coat, black slouch hat and thick felt shoes. When he goes shooting, he means it, too, and wants to get out of it all the pleasure possible."

Partridge Hunting at Brownsville

The *Lancaster Intelligencer* in its Wednesday November 30, 1892 edition reported on a mainland hunt for partridges at Brownsville Plantation, ancestral home of the Upshur family, prominent landowners and public servants. Abel Upshur served as Secretary of State under President Tyler in the 1840s. Tragically, he was killed in 1844 in an explosion aboard the U.S.S. *Princeton* when a cannon was being unveiled to the news media and the public on the Potomac River.

The weather was not suitable for duck hunting, so the president-elect accepted an invitation to go partridge hunting on the upland instead. Brownsville is now the mainland headquarters of The Nature Conservancy.

Mr. Upshur's plantation, which embraces about 1,000 acres, is located across the channel almost directly opposite the southern end of Broadwater Island. It is four miles from Nassawadox, a station on the Cape Charles Railroad, three miles south of Exmore station. The farm is rather marshy along the coast, but slopes upward to a level, dry prairie. Some 300 acres are covered with a good growth of bean brush, which is a favorite refuge for partridge. The game is said to be quite abundant, and good sport is anticipated. The party will be taken from the island to Upshur's farm on the yacht Sunshine. *The distance is about 22 miles. Mr. Cleveland will use his own bird dog, which is said to be a very valuable animal, having cost $500.*

While no definite time has yet been fixed for Mr. Cleveland's departure, it is known that he will remain at least until the first of next week, as he announced his intention of attending divine service at the Broadwater Island church next Sunday. The pastor of this church is Rev. John R. Sturgis, a Methodist Episcopal minister, who permanently resides upon the island with his wife.

Mr. Cleveland Takes His Leave

Mr. Cleveland departed Broadwater Island on Saturday, December 3, 1892, capping off a stay of twelve days. This account is from the *York* (Pa.) *Gazette.*

President-elect Cleveland this afternoon received an invitation from F. N. Pike, manager of the Hygeia Hotel at Old Point Comfort (in Hampton) to spend a day or two at that resort when his visit to Broadwater is completed. In view of the fact that Mr. Cleveland will leave for the north late Sunday evening it is considered improbable that he will accept this invitation. The program for the remainder of Mr. Cleveland's stay upon the island is a final all day ducking expedition tomorrow, a rest indoors on Sunday, and a homeward journey will be at 10:31 o'clock Sunday night.

Final arrangements have been completed for the departure of president-elect Cleveland from Broadwater Island on Sunday. The private car of General Superintendent Kenney of the Philadelphia, Wilmington, and Baltimore Railroad will be brought from Cape Charles to Exmore on Sunday morning and will be side tracked for the reception for Mr. Cleveland and L. Clark Davis, who will accompany him.

The president-elect will be conveyed from there on the steam yacht Sunshine *which will probably reach Willis's Landing shortly after nightfall. The private car conveying the little party northward will be attached to regular train #82, which is due to leave the Exmore station at 10:31 p.m. The scheduled time of this train from Exmore to Jersey City is nine hours and a half, the hour of arrival at the latter place being seven-fifty Monday morning. The present understanding is that Mr. Cleveland will go directly to New York City and not stop at Lakewood, N.J. where his wife is visiting Mrs. Freeman as has been expected. If this program is carried out as arranged, Mr. Cleveland's visit to Broadwater Island will have covered a period of twelve days.*

President Grover Cleveland

The Sunshine

All Aboard the *Sunshine*

A fixture on Broadwater Island in the 1890s was the steam launch *Sunshine*, which was used to ferry guests back and forth between the island and the mainland at Willis Wharf Landing. The boat had a spacious cabin and a small after-deck, so passengers could travel in comfort during blustery weather or enjoy the sea breeze during the warmer months.

The *Sunshine* was also put into use for fishing trips and to ferry guests to other islands or mainland sites. The handwritten caption with this pictures says "returning from a fishing trip."

The *Sunshine* was owned by the Broadwater Club and during its time it transported some distinguished passengers. Grover Cleveland and his entourage traveled on the *Sunshine* during his trips in 1892 and 1893, and the University of Pennsylvania football team commuted to the island in the summer of 1894.

The *Sunshine* made its last trip in 1896. That year storms did a great deal of damage to the barrier islands, washing away the venerable Cobb family hotel on their island retreat south of Broadwater. The *Sunshine* was damaged beyond repair while docked at Broadwater Island.

The *Peninsula Enterprise* of Accomac reported that the "steamer *Sunshine*, used for conveying passengers from this place to Willis Wharf, was sunk at the Government Dock during a gale of wind recently and is a total wreck."

The Sunshine, *with a group of fishermen, enroute to Broadwater Island*

Ivy League Football Comes to Broadwater

The University of Pennsylvania football team won the first of its seven national championships in 1894 with a record of 12-0, and Broadwater Island played an important role. It was standard procedure in those days for major college teams to go on the road for summer practice. Most of the time, teams went to well-known resorts, and the news media would cover the daily workouts and report on the prospects for the teams' fall season. It generated great publicity, and the players no doubt enjoyed the leisure time in the evening when practice had ended.

In 1893 the Quakers had summer practice in Cape May, New Jersey, and the looming presence of the news media kept the team in the headlines for a few weeks, but head coach George Washington Woodruff found that Cape May had its disadvantages. The resort presented too many distractions for a team made up of eager young men, and the news media and the fans in attendance made it impossible to design new plays or to develop strategy beyond the prying eyes of the competition.

Coach Woodruff conferred with some prominent Pennsylvania friends who had Virginia ties, and for the 1894 season this Ivy League team would do something radical. John C. Sims was greatly involved in Penn athletics as president of the University of Pennsylvania Athletic Association, and Clarke Davis was the well-known editor of the *Philadelphia Ledger* newspaper and an advisor to President Grover Cleveland. Sims and Davis conferred with Joe Ferrell, and it was decided to offer the football team full access to Broadwater Island for summer football practice. It was Davis who had orchestrated Cleveland's hunting and fishing trips to Hog Island in 1892 and 1893.

The Broadwater Club was in the summer doldrums in the dog days of 1894; spring shorebird shooting had ended, and the fall waterfowl season was weeks away. The players could bunk in the club house and work out on a grassy meadow in the pine woods. There would be no prying eyes from competing squads, and the team was separated from the news media by ten miles of open water.

The *Philadelphia Times* broke the story in its July 22, 1894 edition: "Officials of the football team and members of the Broadwater Club on Hog Island have reached an agreement on summer football practice to be held at the club for the summer. On Wednesday next Captain Alden Kanipe and trainer (e.g. head coach) George W. Woodruff will leave for the Virginia island and in another week the university football season will have begun."

The players were able to develop offensive and defensive strategy on the grassy practice fields, and they got into shape by running wind sprints on the sandy beach. And, most importantly,

1894 University of Pennsylvania football team

there were no scouts from competing teams looking on. The *Philadelphia Times* praised the effort. "The move to leave Cape May is undoubtedly a wise one," wrote a sports reporter. "When determining the strength of the material in hand it is necessary that the enemy should be kept in the dark. At the Cape it was impossible. At the new stand secrecy is possible since access can only be obtained by the club steamer after a two-hour journey, and the trainers are unlikely to admit a rival. The main benefit is the total absence of anything to distract the player's attention from his work."

The reward was the Quaker's first national championship, even though the team was made up largely of first-year players. Four years later, the captain from that 1894 team, now a doctor, looked back on the season that had begun at Broadwater. "Anyone who has visited that delightful place can easily appreciate the value of the opportunities thus given, and the results of that season's football fully justified the selection of such a place," he told the Philadelphia Times in February 20, 1898. "The players staying on Hog Island were on the scene of action two months before the regular season began, and that exercise and sport was declared by all to be the most beneficial and enjoyable ever spent by them. I can only say that the success of the following season, both from the point of view of a coach and a doctor, was not a mere matter of luck, but was entirely due to the superior condition of the players."

Despite the success, the 1894 pre-season was the Quakers' first and last on Broadwater Island. In 1895 they traveled to a resort on the shores of Lake Ontario in Canada, and in 1896 to Long Island.

The Life-Saving Station and the Wreck of the *San Albano*

Most of the rescues performed by the life-saving service on the Eastern Shore involved ships traveling the coastal routes between New York or Boston and southern ports such as Savannah and Charleston. Many of the rescues were reported in local newspapers, especially when they involved crews and ships from nearby ports. But in 1892 the men of the station at Hog Island rescued a steamship from Spain, saving a crew of twenty-six Spanish sailors, and their act of bravery made world news. Later that year, the king of Spain ordered that the keeper and crew be presented medals of honor recognizing their heroism.

The incident began early on the morning of February 23 when surfman J. R. Dunton was patrolling the beach during a northeast storm. The surf was crashing high on the berm of the beach and sending sea foam to the dune line. The rain was swirling in the wind, mixing with the froth stirred up by the surf, and through the wet darkness, Dunton thought he saw lights. He leaned into the wind and listened, but he could hear nothing but the pounding surf. But then, through the darkness, he saw them again. They were the running lights of a ship, and they were close to the shore. Much too close to the shore.

Dunton quickly reached into his pack for a Coston flare, lighted it, and held it aloft, waving it to get the captain's attention, warning him that his ship was in danger. In less than a minute, the lights disappeared, but Dunton didn't know whether the captain had seen the flare and steered seaward, or if the ship had simply slipped into the darkness once again.

Dunton hurried back to the station and reported what he had seen to keeper John E. Johnson, who went to the lookout tower with his field glasses. At first, Johnson could see nothing, but as dawn approached, the skies slowly went from black to gray, and through the glasses Johnson could make out the masts of the ship over the rims of the sand dunes. He sounded the alarm.

The vessel was a 1,291-ton Spanish steamship built in 1880 called the *San Albano*, sailing out of the port of Bilbao, Spain, heading from New Orleans to Hamburg with a load of cotton, grain, and oil. Laden with cargo, the *San Albano* was drawing nearly 21 feet of water, and she was way too close to shore. The vessel grazed an offshore sandbar, bounced off with the next swell, and when she settled into a trough the captain set his anchors.

The crew of the Hog Island Life-Saving Station pose for a photograph with their new station, circa 1890. The keeper, John E. Johnson, in the foreground, served for twenty-eight years in the position. Sumner Kimball, superintendent of the Life-Saving Service, insisted that the stations should not only be functional, but have architectural details that please the eye. The trim around the door included a carved image of a bird on each side. This one resembles a Black Skimmer, a bird that is abundant in the barrier islands of Virginia. (See insert above.)

The ship was badly off course. The captain's intent was to stop at the port of Hampton Roads to load coal before making the ocean crossing, but the storm made the identification of landmarks difficult, and the captain had passed by Cape Henry and Cape Charles without seeing the lights. The ship came to rest about six miles north of the Hog Island life-saving station, about 500 yards offshore. As the waves came they would lift the ship, and when they retreated she would pound the bottom. Over and over again.

Finally, the *San Albano's* hull gave way and she settled into the trough, the seas breaking over her. Re-floating the vessel was now out of the question; the task now would be to safely remove the crew before the ship broke up. The men of the life-saving service went through endless drills in the station yard, and they kept their equipment in immaculate condition. On the morning of February 23, 1892, they learned the value of those boring drills and endless preparation.

Keeper Johnson ordered the apparatus cart brought to the scene. The cart carried a Lyle gun, powder charges, lines of various sizes, and first aid gear. He also ordered the surf boat and life car, and thus had options. If the Lyle gun failed to secure a lifeline, the men would attempt to reach the ship by boat, an option, but not a pleasant one. It took several hours for the equipment to be moved through sand and water from the station to the site of the grounding, and it was late afternoon by the time the Lyle gun was set up.

The purpose of the gun was to launch a light line to the deck of the stricken ship, have the crew secure it, and then use that line to convey heavier ones. Finally, a breeches buoy would be attached and used to remove the crew one-by-one to safety. The first shot from the Lyle gun fell short, but the second landed on the deck. The Spanish crew, unable to read the instructions for securing the line, did not fasten it properly and when the crew on the beach tightened it, the line gave way. More launches from the Lyle gun fell short, and the rising tide was increasing the range needed to reach the ship.

Meanwhile, seven members of the *San Albano* crew launched the only lifeboat remaining on the ship and miraculously made it to shore. One man went missing when he attempted to swim to shore with the aid of a wooden plank. The good news was that the crew on shore reported that the wreck was still solid and the deck houses were dry.

Keeper Johnson decided to have his men return to the station for food and rest and left a crew of volunteers organized by Reverend J.R. Sturgis to maintain a bonfire on the beach. A horse was left in case the situation changed and the keeper needed to be notified quickly.

After resting for a few hours, the crew returned to find the situation virtually unchanged. The tide was lower, but the *San Albano* was still beyond the range of the Lyle gun. Keeper Johnson had an idea. The Lyle gun is typically fired from the beach, but if it were loaded into the apparatus cart and pushed into the breakers, the range would be reduced. The men attached the gun to the deck of the cart and pushed it through the surf to waist-deep water. The first shot cleared the rail and the Spanish crew this time secured the line properly, and within an hour the life car was removing the remaining nineteen crew members one by one. Of the crew of twenty-seven men, all were saved except one, who had the poor judgement to swim to shore. The men also saved the ship's cat.

The Spanish sailors were taken to the life-saving station where they were fed and given clothes donated by the Women's National Relief Association. They remained at the station for a week, until transportation to the mainland could be arranged. The *San Albano* broke up in the surf of Hog Island, its cargo of cotton, grain, and oil, valued at $120,000, a total loss.

The rescue of the *San Albano* was one of the most notable of the year for the United States Life-Saving Service. The inspector who investigated the incident filed this report: "Great credit is due the keeper and the crew of the Hog Island Station for their brave and persistent efforts, and every man did his whole duty. The people of the island were prompt and ready to assist the life-saving crew in every way possible."

A few months later, the government of Spain honored the life-saving crew, and the king of Spain ordered that medals be made to honor the keeper and each crew member. Those receiving medals and commendations were John E. Johnson, keeper of the station, and surfmen R. C. Joynes, J.R. Dunton, C. F. Carpenter, J. H. DeWald, J. E. Smith, J. K. Carpenter, J. A. Doughty, and William B. Goffigon.

Wrecks were not unusual on the barrier islands, and the ribs of wooden ships were often part of the landscape, a good background for a photograph.

In November of that year, when president-elect Cleveland visited, he personally congratulated the members of the life-saving service. It was Reverend Sturgis, apparently, who told him of the crew's heroic act.

Mary-Russell's Broadwater Island

Joseph and Elise Ferrell's daughter, Mary-Russell, was three when the president-elect visited, and later in her life she recalled sitting on his lap when he visited her home, remembering Cleveland as "a nice jolly fat man."

Mary-Russell spent much of her childhood on Broadwater Island, and the experience had a profound effect on her life. Ironically, although she spent her childhood as an island girl, as an adult she would make her mark in the American Southwest as a noted artist and a champion of the indigenous art of the Hopis and Navajo of northern Arizona. She and her husband, Dr. Harold Colton, co-founded the Museum of Northern Arizona in Flagstaff in 1928, which today remains a thriving institution whose mission is to celebrate the beauty and diversity of the Colorado Plateau.

According to *One Woman's West*, a biography of Mary-Russell written in 1997 by Richard and Sherry Mangum, the Ferrell family spent most of the year on Broadwater Island as they purchased land, saw to the construction of cottages and a clubhouse, and promoted the island as a summer getaway.

"Broadwater Island had a wide sandy beach, a few meadows, and a pine forest," they wrote. "Mary-Russell came to love it, calling it 'my childhood paradise.' Her hair in bangs and often barefoot, she explored the island on the back of a Chincoteague pony; a black servant named Ben Upshur went along to take care of her."

Mary-Russell was apparently an introvert, preferring to provide her own entertainment. She especially enjoyed fishing, and her parents would tie a rope around her waist and anchor it to a bollard on the Broadwater pier, and she would spend many days safely fishing while they conducted business. She enjoyed nature and the outdoors, and her experiences on the island kindled a lifelong appreciation for the natural world.

Hog Island had a forested interior, sand dunes, and about eight miles of beach, and Mary-Russell enjoyed exploring, usually accompanied by various animals. In addition to several dogs, she had lambs, geese, and chickens, which would follow her around as though they were domesticated pets.

Mary-Russell's solitary summer days on Broadwater seem to have awakened her need to express herself through visual art. She attended the Pelham School in Philadelphia and was educated there and by various family members at home. Her father taught her mathematics and her mother history, but her favorite subject was art.

By the end of childhood, Mary-Russell wanted two things out of life, according to her biographers. She wanted to travel to faraway places, and she wanted to become an artist.

Mary-Russell's Chincoteague Pony

When Mary-Russell was fifteen she was accepted into the Philadelphia School of Design for Women, a small but prestigious academy in the city. Unfortunately, misfortune struck the family when Joseph Ferrell suffered a stroke and died on July 14, 1904 at age 64, just weeks before Mary-Russell was to begin classes. By this time, Ferrell had given up the Broadwater project and was concentrating on promoting a fire retardant chemical he had created.

"Joseph Ferrell's finances and health both failed," wrote the Mangums. "Mary-Russell and her mother immediately found themselves in straitened circumstances. Elise had to sell the family furniture, the cottage on Broadwater Island, and other valuable assets to cover their living expenses."

Fortunately, a family friend came to their aid and provided tuition for Mary-Russell to enroll in the Philadelphia School of Design for Women, which was one of the finest art schools in the country and billed itself as America's oldest art school for women.

Mary-Russell was truly in her element in art school. She graduated in four years and was awarded a post-graduate scholarship for a fifth year. During this year of graduate study, Mary-Russell began to travel, joining groups for extended trips to back country destinations in the American west and British Columbia. On one of these trips, she met Dr. Harold S. Colton, a professor of zoology at the University of Pennsylvania. That would be the first of many trips the two would take, mainly to wilderness areas in the western United States. Mary-Russell and Harold were married in Germantown, Pennsylvania, on May 23, 1912, and left for an extended honeymoon at Valley Ranch near Pecos, New Mexico.

The Coltons traveled widely in the southwest, which at the time was frontier territory. They took extended camping trips to wilderness areas, sleeping in tents and preparing their meals over campfires. They discovered Flagstaff on the honeymoon trip, and Harold wrote in his journal, "What a nice place it would be to make a home."

That journal entry would prove to be prophetic. Although the young couple continued to travel and explore the southwest, they eventually settled in Flagstaff. In 1926 they bought a 100-acre tract north of town that they named Coyote Range, and they sold their property back east and claimed Flagstaff as their new home.

By then, the couple had two small boys, Harold had served abroad in the army during World War I, and the Coltons were ready to settle down and become involved in the Flagstaff community. Some of Mary-Russell's art school classmates visited, and the Coltons became involved in studying the art and archaeology of the native people. They became friends with J.C. Clarke, who had promoted the idea of a museum to house artifacts found in the area, and a committee was formed by the Flagstaff Chamber of Commerce to explore the idea.

On May 21, 1928 the Northern Arizona Society of Science and Art was chartered and a board of trustees was chosen. The Coltons were not only on the board, but Harold was named

Mary-Russell and Harold at their wedding and hiking in the desert.

president and director and Mary-Russell appointed curator of art. A small museum was in the Woman's Club building in Flagstaff, and with extensive coverage from the local newspaper, the artifacts began to pour in.

The Coltons assumed day-to-day operation of the museum, and Mary-Russell taught art classes in a former high school. From the beginning, the Coltons turned their attention to the arts and crafts of the native people.

Mary-Russell wrote that the mission of the museum should be to rescue native Hopi arts and crafts: "We believe that our first duty lay with our native population, the Indians of the Painted Desert, our next-door neighbors. We were rather well fitted for this work, having traveled about among the people for years on painting and archaeological trips, and for years having watched with deep regret a gradual degeneration of their unique arts and crafts."

The Mangums wrote that Mary-Russell's most productive years were the 1930s, when she produced her best paintings and made invaluable contributions to the revival and preservation of Hopi art. The collection of indigenous art soon outgrew the space available, and it became necessary to find new quarters. The Coltons donated 29 acres of land on Fort Valley Road, and Harold began sketches of a new museum building. Construction of the first building began in 1934, with funding provided by the Coltons. The museum has expanded greatly over the years, but the mission is unchanged, "to understand

Mary-Russell's family from Kentucky now and then visited the island. She was named for her mother's sister, who went by the name Mary. Mary was married to Lyle Buchanan, a businessman and member of the Kentucky state legislature.

Elise, Mary, and Lyle Buchanan in a wooded area of Broadwater Island.

and share the Colorado Plateau through the study of its natural and cultural heritage."

And so, the island girl whose early years were spent riding a Chincoteague pony on the sandy beaches of Hog Island made the transition from east to west, from seaside islands and bays to the high country of the Colorado Plateau. She and Harold would spend their lives in the West, championing the traditional arts of indigenous people, as Mary-Russell found her own way to visually interpret the landscape and the people of northern Arizona.

Mary-Russell Ferrell Colton lived to be 82, and died at The Bells Lodge in Phoenix on July 16, 1971. By the time of her death, Alzheimer's had swept most of the past from her memory. But her biographers say she would sometimes recall pleasant events from her past. "The things she remembered most were childhood days on her 'Paradise,' Broadwater Island," they said.

Paradise Lost

Joe Ferrell no doubt envisioned Broadwater Island becoming another Atlantic City or Cape May, but that was not to happen. By all accounts, Ferrell was a brilliant promoter, and he and his team of Philadelphia consorts came up with some ingenious plans to grab the headlines. Clarke Davis orchestrated the Grover Cleveland visits in 1892 and 1893, putting Broadwater Island on the front page of newspapers coast to coast. John Sims did the same, using his ties with the athletic department at the University of Pennsylvania to have the football team travel to Broadwater in the summer of 1894 for pre-season practice.

Ferrell had a genius for promotion, but he was tone deaf when it came to the nuances of the market. Broadwater Island offered miles of sandy beach and it seemed to have a world of potential as a resort, but it was far removed from the population centers of the north. Atlantic City and Cape May were easily accessible. The Adirondacks offered respite from the summer doldrums of the city. And an ever-growing roster of Florida resorts attracted northern visitors in the winter, as Henry Flagler developed the east coast of the Sunshine State.

Broadwater was too far north to offer relief from winter weather, and it was too far south to be easily accessible in the summer. The railroad made the island more accessible to northern cities, but getting there still required a day-long train ride, a buggy ride to the Willis Wharf landing, and then a boat ride of several hours across a shallow bay.

While sales did not live up to the intents set forth in the articles of incorporation ("to build thereon dwelling houses, stores, and pleasure resorts including hotels..."), the Broadwater Club still had a following, with a membership of about fifty, most of whom were wealthy Philadelphia businessmen. Investing in property and constructing a dwelling house on remote Broadwater Island did not seem prudent, but membership in a club made up of likeminded friends was different. The club kept the Broadwater development afloat for at least a few years.

Broadwater's distance from population centers was a negative factor, and unforeseen economic turmoil also dimmed the prospects. The Ferrells began buying land on Hog Island in 1886, and they accumulated some 1,700 acres by the time the president-elect visited in 1892. The nationwide publicity generated by Cleveland's visit should have created a ground-swell in land sales, but apparently it did not. The country was on the cusp of a deep depression called the Panic of 1893. Especially hard hit was the railroad industry, and, consequently, steel manufacturing and banking. All three of these sectors were well represented among the Broadwater Club membership.

Many of the businesses and individuals affected by the

recession were involved with the Broadwater project. The Wellman Iron and Steel Company of Chester, Pennsylvania was forced to close in the fall of 1893 because of judgements by banks for non-payment of notes. Samuel T. Wellman, the owner, was a director of the Broadwater Club. The foreclosure caused the layoff of 1200 iron workers. The company was a major supplier of rails for PRR.

In May 1893 the Pennsylvania and Reading Railroad eliminated the jobs of all four vice presidents to save salaries. John Lowher Welsh, a director of the company, was a prominent member of the Broadwater Club.

Frank K. Hipple, owner and president of the Real Estate Trust Company, a Philadelphia bank, took his own life in 1893 after being accused of bank fraud. Hipple was a director of the Broadwater Club.

The Panic of 1893 caused the failure of more than 15,000 businesses, and it became the unfortunate standard by which future recessions would be measured. Many of the business failures involved the railroad industry and providers of goods and services used by the railroad.

The Panic of 1893

The Panic of 1893 stands unique in that it presents an unrivaled record of failures of solvent banks, corporations, firms, and individuals in a country having unsurpassed facilities for production and distribution, and possessing the highest average of civilization and refinement. It was largely a case of financial fright, exaggerated by the extreme sensitivity of the present complex machinery of business, due to the extraordinary increase of railway, steamship, and telegraphic communication between all parts of the world.

The panic's intensity was also increased by the modern evolution and extension of the credit system. Aside from the retail trade, it is demonstrable that more than 95 percent, perhaps as much as 98 percent, of the actual business of the country, involving the transfer of products, is done on credit. It is only within the last twenty years that this complexity and sensitivity of the business world has become so painfully conscious of the rising and falling of the financial barometer.

From the *Public Weekly Opinion*, published in Chambersburg, Pennsylvania, Friday, September 1, 1893. The newspaper has been published in the Cumberland Valley since 1869.

The period of 1892-94 represents perhaps the high point of the Broadwater Island project. In 1892 a new lighthouse was erected, and that spring the Ferrells moved into their cottage designed by T.P. Chandler. The Hog Island Life-saving Service made international headlines when it saved the lives of 26 men aboard a sinking Spanish ship, and in the fall the president-elect visited the island for nearly two weeks. Broadwater

Island was in the news on a regular basis in 1892, and the press coverage continued in 1893 when the president visited again in May. John Sims arranged to have the University of Pennsylvania football team have their summer practice on the island in 1894, and newspapers were reporting from Broadwater for more than a month.

Newspaper coverage of Broadwater slacked off during the latter part of the 1890 decade. On October 13, 1896 a hurricane slammed the Virginia coast, flooding the seaside barrier islands. Cobbs Island, south of Broadwater, suffered major damage. The old hotel, a fixture on the island since Civil War days, was destroyed, and according to the *Richmond Dispatch*, "the structure and its fixtures were carried out to sea." Only three buildings remained on the island, according to the newspaper, two private cottages and the life-saving station.

Broadwater Island also suffered damage, with cottages in low lying areas being made uninhabitable. The club's steam launch, *Sunshine*, was battered by winds and tide and left a wreck as it was moored in the harbor. After the storm of 1896, Joe Ferrell apparently lost interest in developing the island and turned his attention to his engineering and manufacturing projects. On Broadwater Island, Ferrell was working with his aquaculture farm, building oyster beds in the shallow tidal waters around the island. When he was not on the island, Ferrell was spending time in Philadelphia working in his shop and laboratory at 2218 Race Street.

A meeting of Broadwater Island stockholders was called in the summer of 1903 for the purpose of electing officers, and Ferrell was not re-elected president by the members. This ended his tenure as the leader of the company he and his wife Elise created in 1890. Ferrell was replaced by club member James Rawle, a Penn graduate who was president of the J. G. Brill Company of Philadelphia, an engineering firm.

With Ferrell's connection to Broadwater severed, he began working full time in his lab. Ferrell developed a solution that when applied to wood made it virtually fireproof, and on May 19, 1903 he was awarded patent number 728,452 for the solution and the apparatus used to apply it.

In recognition of the achievement, in January 1904 Ferrell was awarded the Elliot Cresson gold medal from the Franklin Institute of Philadelphia, the highest award given for chemical discoveries.

Ferrell channeled his promotional talents from selling island real estate to marketing his fire retardant, which he made from a sulfate of aluminum compound. Ferrell began promoting the product in newspapers around the country and in England.

The January 5, 1904 edition of the *Philadelphia Inquirer* announced that Ferrell had offered to fireproof every theatre in Philadelphia with his new compound. A tragic fire at the Iroquois Theatre in Chicago a year earlier had killed 602 people and injured another 250. Ferrell offered the compound to the city free of charge "except for the cost of the chemical and the labor for applying it."

OFFERS TO MAKE THEATRES SAFE

Inventor Would Coat Free With Fire Resisting Preparation Every City Play House

Joseph L. Ferrell, Holder of Franklin Institute Medal, Makes Proposition to the Mayor

Declaring that he is the inventor of a fire-proof liquid or paint that will render invulnerable to flame any piece of wood or furniture, Joseph L. Ferrell has offered to treat the woodwork of every Philadelphia theatre and render it impervious to fire free of all charge except the actual cost of the material and the labor of applying it.

Mr. Ferrell is a well-known Philadelphia inventor, having been awarded the Elliot Cresson gold medal for chemical mixtures

JOSEPH L. FERRELL.

to render wood impervious to fire by the Franklin Institute in June last. His chemical preparation has its basis in sulphate of aluminum, one of the best non-conductors of heat known to chemists. Besides the fireproof preparation, he is also the inventor of a machine for saturating wooden beams with the fluid. His offer to the Philadelphia playhouse owners is made in the form of an open letter to Mayor Weaver, in which he says:

Offers His Services

"In view of the apprehensions created in the public mind by the appalling disaster at Chicago, and with the conviction that at any moment our own community may be overwhelmed by a like calamity, I am compelled from a sense of duty to offer my services to the public for its protection. I possess the remedy in simple form and of easy application to nullify all fire attack against inflammable materials. I offer to give my services free of cost, and the use of my chemical formulae without any charge, to absolutely render flameless under fire attack, all scenery and stage appliances of the theatres and places of amusement in the city of Philadelphia, as well as the wood of those structures.

"As guarantee that what I offer is solidly based on practical fact, I submit my competency to do what I offer to any committee of experts the Franklin Institute may appoint, and as safe assurance of my disinterestedness and purity of purpose, I respectfully place my proposition and myself at the disposal of his Honor the Mayor of Philadelphia, or any representatives he may designate. This work can be quickly, cheaply and permanently done, and perfect immunity secured for our citizens from fire when they are gathered together in masses for their innocent amusement."

Resists Fire

In his laboratory, at 2218 Race street, yesterday Mr. Ferrell subjected pieces of wood saturated with his fireproof solution to flame from a Bunsen burner that registered 2462 degrees Fahrenheit. After hours of contact the flame blistered the wood and ate a shallow hole into it, but did not cause it to burn with any flame. The demonstration shows that when fire attacks the wood which has been treated with the sulphite of aluminum, the heat causes the aluminum to expand and fill all the wood cells with the non-conductor.

Mr. Ferrell is a Pennsylvanian, a graduate of Yale and a world traveler. He has been working on the fireproof liquid for the past ten years.

He told the *Philadelphia Inquirer*, "In view of the apprehension created in the public mind by the appalling disaster at Chicago, and with the conviction that at any moment our own community may be overwhelmed by a like calamity, I am compelled from a sense of duty to offer my services to the public for its protection."

Ferrell never got to fireproof Philadelphia theatres. That summer he suffered a stroke and died on July 15, 1904, at age sixty-four, when Mary-Russell was fifteen years old. Ferrell no longer controlled the Broadwater Club at the time of his death, but he still owned property on the island, and he remained a principal stockholder of both the Broadwater and Parramore Land and Improvement Companies. In his will, recorded in September 1904 in the office of the Northampton County Clerk of Court, lifetime rights to Ferrell's first cottage went to Miranda Hamlin, and lifetime rights to the "Robbins House" went to Emma Albright. Both Hamlin and Albright were family members. Shares of Broadwater and Parramore stock were left to several relatives, and the remainder of his estate, which included the cottage designed by T. P. Chandler, went to his wife, Elise. Ferrell was buried in Louisville, Kentucky, in Cave Hill Cemetery, the Houston family cemetery.

Even though the Ferrells were no longer involved in running Broadwater, the club and all that was associated with it lived on for several years after his death. The Broadwater Land and Improvement Company, whose capital stock sold for \$5.00

a share in 1890, was dissolved by the Virginia Corporation Commission on November 22, 1921, and its assets distributed to shareholders. A $5.00 share was worth $2.05. In 1922 a charter was issued to the Broadwater Island Land Company, a group from Richmond that used the mainland lodge Ferrell built on Brownsville for their duck hunting trips.

The Ferrell family, no longer members of the Broadwater Club, still owned property on the island and they visited it now and then. Mary-Russell spent much of her childhood on the island and loved to return as an adult, although her travels in the west left her little time to do so.

There obviously was some enmity between the Ferrells and the members of the club. Mary-Russell visited in April 1911 when she was twenty-two and wrote to Harold Colton from the mainland lodge at Brownsville, which she referred to as The Hummocks. She was planning to leave for the island the next day, but wanted to do some canoeing in the seaside marshes before she left. Canoes were stored there, but she was hesitant to use them because they were the property of the club. "It is still tantalizing to think, however, that there are two nice canoes under the house, just begging to be used; but alas, they belong to "Club Members," so therewith, high and dry, literally," she wrote.

Mary-Russell's trip to Broadwater in the spring of 1911might have been her final visit. It is the last one documented by letters. She and Harold were married a year later, and thus began her life in America's Southwest.

According to Whitelaw's history, the hunting club closed in 1929 shortly after the stock market crash. Whitelaw reported that a 1924 survey showed 286 acres under club ownership.

The peak years of the Broadwater development came during the decade of the 1890s. Joe Ferrell worked closely with John Sims and Clarke Davis and others of the Pennsylvania Railroad fraternity. Sims's unexpected death in 1901 must have been a blow for Ferrell. The two had worked closely and Sims had done a great deal to promote Broadwater. Sims was stricken with appendicitis in December 1900 and was hospitalized and had surgery. His recovery seemed to go well, and then on January 6, 1901 he suffered a heart attack and died while still in the hospital. Sims's death likely contributed to Ferrell's loss of interest in the project.

Clarke Davis, another close friend and Broadwater promoter, became ill in 1903 and could no longer participate in the business affairs of the club. Davis died in 1904, just a few weeks after Ferrell passed.

The demise of the Broadwater Island development was brought about by a tapestry of misfortunes. The deep recession brought on by the Panic of 1893 greatly affected American industry during the waning years of the 19th century, especially the railroads. While the opening of the railroad on the Eastern Shore in 1884 greatly improved the accessibility of the islands to visitors, Hog Island was still separated from the mainland by ten miles of open water. Other beach resorts were closer to northern

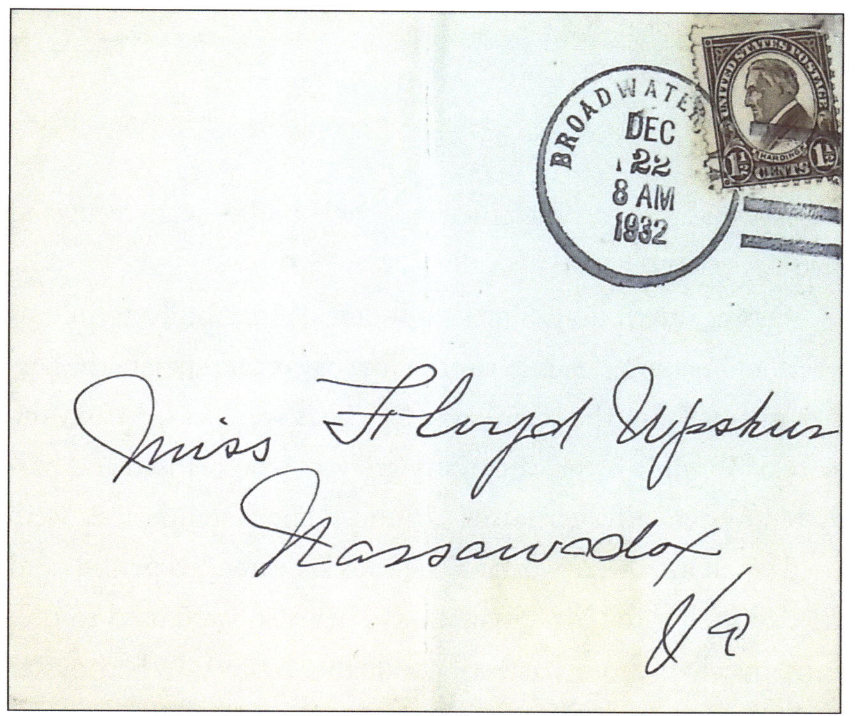

cities and were more easily reached. Broadwater was situated to attract the adventurous, not the masses.

The decade of the 1890s was a special one for Virginia's Eastern Shore and Broadwater Island, as the new railroad ushered in a modern era. Those years featured presidential visits, Ivy League football, feverish coverage from national media, and formidable changes in the lifestyle of local people. Broadwater was a light that flashed brilliantly, and then dimmed.

Charles Sterling, a Hog Island resident who worked as an assistant lightkeeper, wrote a small book about the island and its people in 1903. Broadwater barely got a mention. When Sterling listed the major landowners of the island, he named Capt. George W. Doughty, Nancy Kelly, and Mr. Ferrill (sic), of Philadelphia. The name of the island reverted to Hog Island, although in Sterling's opinion, the island should have been named Machipongo, reflecting its Native American past.

Sterling does say that, "For many years it (the island) has been the favorite rendezvous of ex-president Cleveland and his coterie of choice spirits."

And of the Broadwater Club he writes, "The Sportsman's Club, owing to a lack of harmony amongst its members, has not proven a success."

The Broadwater Land and Improvement Company was dissolved by the Virginia Corporation Commission in 1921, but the name Broadwater lived on for years. Mail sent from the island post office wore the Broadwater postmark for more than a decade.

The Storm of '33

In August 1933 a strong hurricane formed in the tropics and made its way north. It came ashore on the Outer Banks of North Carolina and weakened as it moved up the coast. But as the eye of the storm passed over Norfolk and entered the bay, the storm re-gained strength and slowed in its northerly movement. It pounded the coast of Virginia and Maryland for two days, creating tidal flooding like no one had seen before. Hurricanes were not given names until 1950, but local people know all about the Storm of '33. It was the storm of the century.

In 1933 we did not have weather satellites and radar to track approaching storms, so many were unaware that a storm was on the way. Capt. Thomas Phillips and Revell Matthews of Willis Wharf were working in their oyster watch house in Hog Island Bay on Wednesday morning, August 23. It had been raining and blowing, but they had no idea what was in store for them. Although the storm was a minimal hurricane when it came to wind speed, it created the greatest storm surge ever recorded on the Virginia coast.

The tide crested at nearly ten feet above mean low water, twice what a normal high tide would be. It was as though the tide had risen to its normal high, but instead of ebbing, continued to rise for another six hours. The tide rose like a swollen river, and before the two men could retreat to the mainland, they were swept away on the currents. Their bodies were recovered two days later.

Oyster watch houses were wooden shelters built on pilings overlooking oyster beds in the shallow bays that separate the barrier islands from the mainland. The beds were leased from the state of Virginia by private oyster growers who planted and harvested oysters on their leased grounds. The watch houses were used when men were working the beds for extended periods and needed shelter for overnight stays. They also were used to prevent poachers from harvesting valuable oysters. When oyster beds were ready to be harvested, growers often spent the night in the watch house with a shotgun handy.

Capt. Phillips and Revell Matthews were not the only two men on watch house duty when the storm struck. Ten men went missing that day, including four members of the Lafferty family. Miraculously, they were discovered clinging to the ruins of the watch house when the storm subsided.

George Cobb, a member of the well-known Cobbs Island family, was lost in the storm. He apparently ignored the men of the Life-Saving Service who offered to transport him to safety.

South of Hog Island, in the fishing village of Oyster, Mrs. Jessie Davis retreated to the roof of her home when the tidal waters flooded the interior and began creeping up the walls. She

Volume LIII ACCOMAC C. H., VA., SATURDAY, SEPTEMBER 2, 1933 Number 11

CHECK UP SHOWS 5 PERSONS LOST LIVES IN STORM LAST WEEK

Damage To Waterfront Business Places Is About As Reported In Last Issue

HEAVY LOSS REPORTED AT OYSTER

Narrow Escapes From Drowning Are Recorded From Several Sections Of Shore

A more complete check-up of the destruction wrought on the Eastern Shore last week by the northeast storm on Tuesday and Wednesday shows that 5 persons lost their lives, numbers of persons had narrow and thrilling escapes from their homes adjoining the seaside of the peninsula or on the Island and marshes adjoining, and the property damage will run into several million dollars. There is hardly a seaside farm from the Maryland line to Cape Charles that was not damaged and in most instances they were flooded by salt water, homes and outbuildings were

Some Scenes After Storm Last Week

Top row, reading left to right: Boat in front of Johnson's store at Willis Wharf; picture taken from porch of Hotel Wachapreague looking toward Fosque's store. Bottom row, left to right: Scene at dock at Franklin City; Metompkin Coast Guard Station; Boats and lumber thrown up in yard of W. E. Walker, at Willis Wharf.

HALLWOOD NATIONAL BANK REOPENS 100% NEXT TUESDAY

Comptroller Of Currency Announces That Conservatorship Ends September 5, 9 A. M.

WORKING ON LIMITED BASIS SINCE MARCH

Secretary Of Treasury Approves Reorganization Plans And Issues License

The Hallwood National Bank, which has been open on a limited basis since the President's order of March 4, closed all of the banks of this country, will re-open 100% next Tuesday, September 5th, at 9 a. m. The Comptroller of the Currency announced on Thursday that he had approved the plans for the reorganization of the bank and that the conservatorship will end at 9 a. m., next Tuesday, when the affairs of the bank will be returned to the Board of Directors and the bank will be allowed to resume its operations un-

took along her two-year-old son, who clung to her as the water rose. The child was torn away by a wind-driven swell.

A coast guardsman drowned on Wallops Island when the station was washed into the sea. The unidentified guardsman was attempting to escape the island in a boat when he was washed away. Reports from Public Landing, Maryland, said that the coast guard boat washed ashore there, and one of the buildings from the station could be seen floating in the bay.

The Wallops Island Club sustained severe damage, and members of the club and their guests were forced to lash themselves to trees to avoid being washed away.

On the bayside, in Hacks Neck, 66-year-old William Cutler was killed when a limb fell from a tree and pinned him beneath the floodwaters.

On Hog Island, seventy-one residents took shelter in the life-saving station as their homes were battered, many of them

Peninsula Enterprise.

Volume LIII — ACCOMAC C. H., VA., SATURDAY, AUGUST 26, 1933 — Number 10

OVER $1,000,000 DAMAGE BY STORM

STORM INTERRUPTS N. R. A. WORK ON EASTERN SHORE

General Assembly Votes Repeal Election For October 3rd; Both Branches Unanimous In Ordering Referendum. Set Date Of Convention For Oct. 25

ACCOMACK COUNTY WHITE SCHOOLS OPEN THURSDAY, SEPT. 14 Superintendent Wise Completes

Young Democrats Honor F.B. Waters At Richmond Meeting Elect Him Chairman Of First District, Of Rules And Delegate To Kansas City

Eastern Shore Water Fronts At Franklin City, Eastern Side Chincoteague, Wachapreague, Willis Wharf, Quinby Are Swept By Heaviest Storm Ever To Visit Section ...Many Seaside Farms Partly Under Water...Crops Destroyed By Wind And Water.

destroyed. This number would probably have been close to the total population of Hog Island at the time. It had been dropping steadily from a total of 173 individuals listed in the 1910 federal census.

The severity of the storm was well documented by newspapers. The following account appeared in the Saturday, August 26 edition of the *Norfolk Virginian-Pilot.*

Tales of narrow escapes were legion. Mr. and Mrs. Larrimore Cushman, of Mockhorn Island, in Magothy Bay, were rescued by Coast Guards after they had clung for seven hours to the flagpole on the roof of their lodge. The island -- drained, diked, and converted into a game preserve -- is one of the show places on the Atlantic seaboard. Cattle and other livestock on the island were almost annihilated, a few escaping by swimming to the mainland.

It was not known here today whether any of the famous Chincoteague Island ponies, which had taken refuge on Assateague Island, had escaped. Hundreds of cattle, grazing on the low-lying marshes on the seaside, were unable to reach the highland, and were drowned.

Five new inlets were opened between Assateague Island and Ocean City, Md.

Damage to farm crops, especially to corn, is incalculable. The fodder was ripped into shreds, and in some instances whole fields were beaten into the mud. Even the low-lying sweet potato vines were stripped of leaves, and the tomato crop, grown for canneries, is practically a total loss.

On scores of farms, the sea rose so rapidly that the dwellers could not get their automobiles out, but used carts and light wagons to flee to higher land. Many turned loose their horses and cattle to fend for themselves.

Fishing boats and pleasure craft were washed into the main streets of many of the towns. Houses were unroofed, and in many cases turned end over end. Many families living on the ocean side were forced to vacate their farms at peril of their lives, some escaping in boats.

On Wallops Island, 45 persons were rescued and taken to a place of apparent safety by the Coast Guard, but the steadily rising water forced them to take to the trees, where they lashed themselves with sections of rope. For 36 hours, women watched the breakers roll through the woods and felt their precarious refuges shake, before rescuers could reach them.

Coast Guard stations at Metompkin, Wachapreague, Cobbs Island, and Wallops Beach were reported abandoned.

Storm damage in Wachapreague showing fishing boats washed up on Main Street across from the Wachapreague Hotel.

The Storm of '33 changed Hog Island. The days of the Broadwater Club were over before the storm struck, but the flood waters likely destroyed all evidence of its prior life. The cottages, not designed to withstand storms, were gone, and likely the clubhouse and the elaborate refuge designed by T. P. Chandler as well. The only surviving structure associated with Broadwater was the mainland lodge on the Brownsville farm, where its remains could be seen in the marshy hummocks for many years.

And the Storm of '33 changed the native islanders as well. It was not just that homes were lost and damaged, boats destroyed, livestock lost. Hog Islanders were used to storms – dealing with nor'easters was part of island living – but this was different.

The island had been under siege for days. Friends and relatives had been lost, and there had been funerals, too many funerals. Ten people had perished that morning on Virginia's Eastern Shore, twenty-one on the Delmarva Peninsula. Hog Island no longer felt safe. It no longer felt like home.

The Exodus

And so, they began to leave, not in a great mass, but one by one, family by family. And they took their houses with them.

The houses were jacked up and logs were placed under them and they were rolled onto barges called oyster monitors. It was slow and tedious work, but the men of Hog Island soon became good at it. Houses were moved to locations all over the Eastern Shore, but most went to nearby Willis Wharf and Oyster. A community east of the Willis Wharf harbor today is called Little Hog Island. All the homes there came from the island.

Most of the homes were moved in the late 1930s, and the storm of '33 is generally given as the cause. But people were leaving before then. L. E. Doughty's family moved to New Jersey around 1923. In his narrative about growing up on Hog Island, he mentions that the Hog Island school had only seven grades. For him to complete high school, his mother moved to the mainland, rented a home, and enrolled him in the Willis Wharf school.

Life on the island had to have been harsh, but the rough spots have been worn smooth by the passage of time. We tend to be sentimental about our past, and no one remains who can tell us exactly what life was like on Hog Island. We have some written records, but these are tales drawn from the clouds of selective memory. No one mentions the mosquitos and green-head flies. There is no envy of cousins on the mainland who have electric lights and indoor plumbing and movies to go to on Saturday nights. No one writes of the child who died of appendicitis because he could not reach a hospital in time.

The people who lived on Hog Island were special. Tough. Resourceful. Resilient. Hard working. They embodied the last of the wilderness spirit. Their lives were firmly attached to the land and the sea. There was a constant awareness among them of the place where they lived. The tides. The seasons. The daily nuances of the natural world. They lacked some of the conveniences of life that we find necessary today, but by another measure they were wealthy people. They lived a life of uncluttered simplicity, dependent upon themselves and their neighbors. Their wants were few, and their needs were modest.

The first permanent resident on Hog Island was probably Peter Dowty, who settled around 1750. The last was Southy "Sud" Bell, a tall, lanky oysterman and banjo picker who stuck it out in a two-room shack with his son Milford until both left in the late 1940s. Sud moved to Corpus Christi, Texas, where he died on January 30, 1949. He is buried in Belle Haven Cemetery.

The lives of Peter Dowty and Sud Bell frame another time and another place that we are unlikely to ever see again.

Southy "Sud" Bell was the last resident of Hog Island and was known as a banjo player.

This aerial photo of Hog Island was taken in the 1930s during the declining days of the community. Many of the dwellings appear to be vacant. A structure with three dormers in the upper-right portion of the picture could be the remains of the old clubhouse.

Coda

"...the end of slavery required new economic, social, and political arrangements. As Eastern Shoremen struggled with these challenges, Northern capitalists eyed investment opportunities on the conquered peninsula."

Brooks Miles Barnes
Steam and Steel – The Eastern Shore of Virginia 1870-1884

Development of the Virginia barrier islands was very much a process described by historian Brooks Miles Barnes in his 2024 book. The Broadwater development on Hog Island was a product of the rail era, which began in 1884 with the opening of the New York, Philadelphia and Norfolk Railroad. Prior to the railroad, in the years following the Civil War, shallow draft sidewheelers made the wharfs and landings of Eastern Shore creeks accessible to northern markets in Baltimore, launching a period of economic growth and social change. The railroad amplified these changes, linking the industrial north with the agricultural south, and it widened the umbrella of economic opportunity. The steamship era strengthened a bond between Eastern Shore people and Baltimore, but the railroad introduced a new set of suitors, as commercial interests in Philadelphia, New York, and Boston became enamored of the fertile fields and productive waters of the peninsula. The Eastern Shore became famous for a wide variety of specialty foods, ranging from salty seaside oysters and terrapins, to strawberries and sweet potatoes.

As the railroad era blended into the steamship era, it created revolution within the landscape. Shipping gave rise to dozens of wharfs and landings that drew people and commerce down the necks of the peninsula on both the seaside and bayside. Until 1884, the central ridge of the peninsula, called the mid-woods, was terra incognita. But once rails were laid, once the first carlot was shipped by land instead of sea, an exodus began. Towns and villages began to spring up in the mid-woods, usually where a road crossing the peninsula intersected with the rail line. The wharfs and landings competed successfully with rail for years, but ships eventually gave way to rail, and rail was supplanted by the motor truck. The famous Old Bay Line continued its overnight passenger and freight service until 1962, ending just prior to the opening of the Chesapeake Bay Bridge-Tunnel in 1964. The last passenger train ran on January 12, 1958, and freight service ended in 2018. A biking and hiking trail has been constructed along much of the old railroad right-of-way.

A number of gunning clubs were on the barrier islands, often in stations abandoned by the coast guard and sold to private interests. But four well-established clubs were organized in the late 1880s, and these lasted many years and became part of the history and tradition of the Virginia coast. All four were, to some degree, a product of the railroad.

Broadwater Island, as we have seen, is one that would qualify as an investment opportunity in the eyes of Northern capitalists. Broadwater was created to grab a market share, to generate a profit for shareholders. Broadwater was the spark in the eye of Joe Ferrell, but he brought along with him a team of promoters and profiteers. Broadwater was the work of Philadelphians, most of whom were associated with the Pennsylvania Railroad and/or the University of Pennsylvania.

Another group from Pennsylvania created a club on Wallops Island, but this club concentrated more on family outings than self-promotion and profit. The Wallops Island Association was formed in 1889 when its members purchased Wallops Island for $8,000. In the summer of 1890, they contracted with Chincoteague builder William Conant to build a two-storied clubhouse. On May 16, 1891 Conant presented them the keys to a handsome new facility, and thus began the first summer season of the Wallops Island Club.

Unlike many of the other clubs, Wallops did not focus on waterfowl hunting, and it operated mainly during the spring and summer months. Visitors frequently included family groups, and the children were welcome. Local newspapers would make note of the opening of the club each spring.

The Wallops Island Club was organized and managed by an association of businessmen, so it is not surprising that the club was governed like any good corporation. The shareholders held annual meetings, voted on business matters, approved budgets, and elected officers. The association operated for some sixty years.

Records of the annual meetings and the statements of assets and liabilities still exist, providing a vivid picture of the business side of running a barrier island club. The annual meeting of the association in 1928 was held on October 1 at the Bellevue-Stratford Hotel in Philadelphia. At that time the club had a net worth of $77,907.63. Assets included 3,000 acres of land at $15 an acre, a clubhouse valued at $25,000, and other improvements including a stable and ice house, servant quarters and garage, boathouses, pumps, and docks. Floating assets included three launches, and livestock numbered 200 sheep at $4 and 100 ponies at $20. The only liabilities were several on-demand notes from banks.

Other Pennsylvanians, most of whom were from Pittsburgh, chartered a club on Revels Island, a marshy inner island near the south end of Parramore Island. The club was chartered on September 23, 1887 as the Old Dominion Gunning and Angling Association. The name was changed to the Revels Island Club in 1893.

The association owned a vast tract of marshland southwest of Parramore consisting of Revels Island and nearby Sandy Island, which lay south and west of Revels Island Bay. These inner islands are east of Upshur Neck, which extends north and south like a green finger of upland separating Machipongo River and Upshur Bay.

Membership in the club was by purchase of stock, with each share assessed a certain amount each year to maintain and improve the property held in common, which consisted of a club house, boat house, docks, barns, pastures, and quarters for employees and guides. Membership was open to anyone who bought shares, and each May, in Pittsburgh, shares would be sold at public auction that had been forfeited because the annual assessment was in arrears. The Revels Island Club had a membership of around one hundred, depending upon the annual rate of attrition.

A ridge of high land ran along the spine of Revels Island, roughly north and south, pretty much parallel to the beach on nearby Parramore. The club built its common areas along this ridge, and lots were sold to individuals, who built cottages of their own. This area was just west of the south end of Parramore, tucked behind a sandy hook on the north edge of Quinby Inlet; a channel called The Swash separates Revels from the barrier beach.

A well-known member of the club was George Shiras, III, who came from a prominent Pittsburgh family and whose father was a Supreme Court justice. Shiras was himself a lawyer and politician, having served in the U.S. Congress, but he also enjoyed hunting, fishing, and was a keen naturalist. In Congress, he helped lay the foundation for legislation that would become the Migratory Bird Law of 1916 and the Migratory Bird Treaty Act of 1918. He also was a nationally known wildlife photographer, and *National Geographic* magazine once devoted an entire issue to his work. His two-volume book, *Hunting Wildlife with Camera and Flash Light*, includes two chapters on his days at Revels Island. Shiras visited Revels Island for nearly forty years.

Not far from Revels Island, in a high marsh that separates the mainland from Parramore Island, stood the Accomack Club, whose members were New York businessmen. Unlike the Revels Island Club, which welcomed anyone who purchased stock, the Accomack Club was very exclusive. The club was chartered on January 12, 1887 and was limited to 35 members. To become a member, an applicant had to be approved by a unanimous vote of existing members, pay an initiation fee of $100, and then pay annual dues of $75.

When the NYP&N railroad opened in 1884, it made the seaside clubs of the Eastern Shore accessible from northern cities. Visitors would board the train in New York or Wilmington in the morning and arrive in Keller that afternoon, where they would get transportation to Wachapreague to catch the launch to the islands. The Keller station served both the Revels Island Club and the Accomack Club, and the news media regularly recorded the arrivals and departures.

The curious thing about the Accomack Club is its connection to the Fulton Fish Market in New York, which was built in 1822 beneath what is now the base of the Brooklyn Bridge on the East River. The seven men who founded the Accomack Club were involved with the Fulton Market, and several of the members were officers of both the market and the club. In the 1890s Samuel Stoner was president of the club. He also was president of the Fulton Fish Market. Benjamin West also served as president of the club in the 1890s. He was secretary of the Fulton Fish Market.

Another curious aspect about the club is the way it fully embraced the Eastern Shore community. Most of the gunning clubs employed local people as guides, cooks, and caretakers, but the Accomack Club went to great lengths to ingratiate itself with the people and the government of Accomack County.

Each May, around the time we celebrate Memorial Day today, the club would hold a regatta in which local sailors would compete for prizes such as silver tea sets, gold pieces, parlor clocks, and sewing machines. The regattas attracted hundreds of people to the seaside east of Wachapreague, and a great banquet would be held and speeches would be made. Officers of the club would eloquently sing the praises of Accomack County, and local dignitaries would extend a warm welcome to their northern friends. Music would be part of the celebration, and the Cashville Cornet Band was a favorite.

The spring regatta was a special social occasion for Accomack County, and the local newspapers gave full coverage to both the sailboat races and the celebrations that attended them.

This surprisingly felicitous relationship between New York City businessmen and Accomack County farmers and fishermen could be explained by noting that these folks had a strong common interest. The Eastern Shore was one of the most productive seafood sources on the east coast in the 1890s, sending to northern markets thousands of gallons of oysters, as well as diamondback terrapins, which were extremely valuable and highly sought after by restaurants.

Polk Lang, a local ship captain and businessman, had an oyster shucking house on Folly Creek that employed more than fifty shuckers during the season. It is likely that the regattas, the valuable prizes, the banquets, and the welcoming nature of the club were designed to foster a close relationship with important suppliers of seafood for the Fulton Market. A newspaper story covering a regatta in the 1890s listed Capt. Polk Lang of Folly Creek among the winners. He received a silver pitcher for his first place finish. And regarding the Accomack Club, we have a case, perhaps, of Northern capitalists bearing gifts.

Acknowledgements

This book is the result of an unlikely partnership between two small museums that are miles apart, both literally and figuratively. The mission of the Museum of Northern Arizona is to foster the beauty and diversity of the Colorado Plateau through preserving the region's natural and cultural heritage. It is located in Flagstaff, Arizona.

The Eastern Shore of Virginia Barrier Islands Center is in Machipongo, Virginia, some 2,250 miles east of Flagstaff, on the Virginia coast. The mission of the Barrier Islands Center is to preserve and perpetuate the history and culture of the barrier islands of Virginia.

The link between these two museums is a woman named Mary-Russell Ferrell Colton, one of the most talented artists to have worked in America's Southwest in the 20th century. Mary-Russell and her husband, Dr. Harold Colton, were co-founders of the Museum of Northern Arizona. Mary-Russell spent her childhood on Hog Island on the Virginia coast, and she carried a lifetime of love for coastal islands with her when she migrated west. The photographs in this book capture what she called her "Childhood Paradise."

This book would not have been possible without the cooperation of the Museum of Northern Arizona, especially their archivist, Lily Elbaum, who made some two hundred scans of images in photo albums in the museum collection. The photographs of Broadwater Island are from the collection of the museum, unless otherwise noted.

We also are indebted to the staff of the Northampton County Clerk of Court and to the deputy clerk, Morgan Doughty, whose family were among the original settlers on Hog Island. Morgan was a great help in finding deeds, maps, and other documents pertaining to the island history.

We thank the Philadelphia Athenaeum and archivist Kristina Wilson for the architectural rendering of the Ferrell Cottage on Hog Island made by the noted architect Theophilus P. Chandler and for the photograph of Mr. Chandler. We thank the alumnae office of the University of Pennsylvania for biographical information on persons associated with the Broadwater project and for the photograph of the 1894 football team. The maps we used were courtesy of the David Rumsey Map Center of Stanford University. Thanks also to the Eastern Shore of Virginia Heritage Center, Jazmine Collins and archivist Luke Kelly. Thanks to Dr. Martin Mayer, Dr. Brooks Miles Barnes, Sally Dickinson, Kristen Dennis, and the staff at the Barrier Islands Center. Thanks also to Susan Deaver Olberding's collection of lettters of Mary-Russell, *...going sketching now*, will write again soon., published in 2020 by Fort Valley Publishing.

Two web sites were invaluable in accessing newspapers and other publications that held a wealth of information on the times and places associated with Broadwater Island. They include *Countryside Transformed*, a collaborative effort of the Eastern Shore Public Library and the Virginia Center for Digital History of the University of Virginia, which has a wealth of Eastern Shore material ranging from newspapers to legal documents. Covering a broader landscape is the website *Newspapers.com*, which provided access to many Pennsylvania newspapers that covered the people and events of Broadwater Island.

And last but certainly not least, I need to thank my wife Lynn, my partner and co-author, whose research and organizational skills made this book possible. She is an editor, a mentor, and an all around history detective who kept me on the right trail.

Index

A

Accomac 53
Accomack Club 81, 82
Accomack County 82
Across Levels 29, 30
Albright, Emma 69
Alderson, William C. 19
Altoona Tribune 20
architect/architecture 5, 10, 12, 15, 20, 83
Assateague Island 42, 45, 74
A.T. Mears and Company 11

B

Bacon, George V. 11
Barnes, Brooks Miles 10, 79, 83
Barrier Islands Center 4, 5, 83
Bayard family 20, 21, 22, 24, 25
Bayard, James P. 21, 27
Bayard, Thomas F. 20, 21
Bell, Southy "Sud" 76, 77
Bibby, Edmund 42
Biddle, Clement 27
broadwater 7, 24
Broadwater Club 18, 19, 20, 23, 24, 46, 47, 48, 49, 53, 54, 66, 67, 69, 70, 71, 75
Broadwater Island 1, 2, 3, 4, 5, 7, 8, 9, 10, 12, 15, 19, 20, 21, 23, 24, 25, 26, 29, 45, 46, 48, 49, 50, 51, 53, 54, 56, 61, 63, 65, 66, 67, 68, 70, 71, 75, 79, 80, 83, 84
Broadwater Island Land Company 70
Broadwater Land and Improvement Company 3, 9, 11, 23, 46, 49, 69, 71
Broadwater Oyster Association 19, 23, 48
Browne, Orris A. (Captain) 18
Brownsville (farm or plantation) 18, 50, 70, 75
Buchanan, Lyle 65
Buchanan, Mary-Russell 38, 39, 65
Burn Hill 29

C

Cape Charles City 46
Cape Charles (nautical) 59
Cape Charles Railroad 50
Cape Charles (town) 50
Cape Henry 59
Cape May 15, 54, 56, 66
Carpenter, C. F. 60
Carpenter, J. K. 60
Cashville Cornet Band 82
Cave Hill Cemetery 69
Chandler, Theophilus P. 5, 12, 13, 14, 19, 20, 46, 47, 67, 69, 75, 83
Chase, Howard 49
Cherry Ridge 29
Cherrystone Landing 1
Chincoteague Island 11, 42, 74, 80
Chincoteague pony 61, 62, 65, 74
Churris, Wescoat 10
Clarke, J. C. 63
Clark, George 42
Cleveland, Grover (President) 5, 7, 19, 20, 21, 23, 34, 43, 46, 48, 49, 50, 51, 53, 54, 60, 61, 66, 71
clubhouse 3, 15, 16, 17, 18, 24, 27, 47, 48, 49, 75, 78, 80
coast guard 73, 79
Cobb family 1, 53
Cobb, George 72
Cobbs Island 7, 8, 15, 68, 72, 75
Colton family 63, 64
Colton, Harold S. (Doctor) 61, 63, 64, 65, 70, 83
Colton, Mary-Russell Ferrell 3, 4, 15, 40, 61, 62, 63, 64, 65, 69, 70, 83
Conant, William 80
cricket 10, 15, 19, 23
Cushman, Larrimore and wife 74
Cutler, William 73

D

Davis, Henry L. 27
Davis, L. Clarke 11, 19, 20, 24, 27, 41, 46, 48, 51, 54, 66, 70
Davis, Mrs. Jessie 72
Davis, Rebecca Harding 27
DeWald, J. H. 60
Doughty, Ann 10
Doughty, Eli 10
Doughty family 1, 42
Doughty, George W. (Captain) 43, 45, 71

Doughty, J. A. 60
Doughty, L. E. 45, 76
Doughty, Morgan 83
Doughty, William J. 10
Dowty, Peter Jr. 42, 76
Dunne, H. W. 27
Dunton, J. R. 57, 60
DuPont, Sophie 12, 15

E

Elbaum, Lily 4, 5, 83
Exmore (landing or station) 8, 42, 48, 50, 51

F

Ferrell Cottage 83
Ferrell, Elise Houston 2, 3, 10, 15, 19, 36, 38, 39, 40, 61, 63, 65, 68, 69
Ferrell family 3, 4, 5, 11, 12, 14, 15, 16, 17, 19, 46, 47, 61, 66, 67, 69, 70
Ferrell, Joseph L. 1, 2, 3, 4, 7, 8, 9, 10, 11, 15, 18, 19, 20, 24, 40, 41, 46, 48, 49, 54, 61, 63, 66, 68, 69, 70, 71, 80
Ferrell, Mary-Russell. *See Colton, Mary-Russell Ferrell*
Fig Orchard 29, 31
fireproofing/fireproof materials 48, 63, 68, 69
Fisher, Sydney G. 23, 27
Floyd, John 42
Folly Creek 82
football 2, 20, 26, 53, 54, 55, 56, 66, 68, 71, 83
Fraley, Joseph C. 27
Franklin Institute of Philadelphia 68
Frothingham, Theodore 18, 27
Fulton Fish Market 81, 82

G

Goffigon, William B. 60
Government Dock 53
Government Road 35
Grandma Robbins 36
Green, Kane 49
Griscomb, Clement A. 27

H

Hacker, William 18, 23, 27
Hacks Neck 73
Hamlin, Miranda 69
Harper's Weekly 47
Harrison, Benjamin (President) 46
Hipple, Frank K. 19, 27, 67
Hogg Island. *See Hog Island*
Hog Island 1, 3, 4, 7, 8, 9, 10, 15, 24, 29, 32, 33, 34, 37, 39, 40, 42, 43, 44, 45, 46, 48, 54, 56, 57, 60, 61, 65, 66, 70, 71, 72, 73, 74, 75, 76, 77, 78, 79, 83
Hog Island Bay 72
Hog Islanders 42, 75
Hog Island Life-saving Service 58, 59, 67
Hog Island lighthouse 9, 33
Hog Island Station 60
Hog Island Virginia 7
Hopi 61, 64
Houston, Elise. *See Ferrell, Elise Houston*
Houston family 69
Houston, Russell 10
Hunting Wildlife with Camera and Flash Light 81
Hunt, Thomas 42

J

Jayne, Henry laBarre 27
Jefferson, Charles B. 48
Jennings, William 5, 20, 29
J. G. Brill Company 68
Johnson, John E. 57, 58, 59, 60
Joynes, R. C. 60

K

Kanipe, Alden 54
Keller 81
Keller station 81
Kelly, Luke 83
Kelly, Nancy 71
Kendall, G. S. 19
Kenney, [no first name] (General Superintendent) 50
Kershaw, Mary 4

L

Lafferty family 72
Lancaster Intelligencer 20, 50
Lang, Polk (Captain) 82
Levring, William M. 18
life-saving crew 60
life-saving service 57, 59, 60
Life-Saving Service 58, 72
life-saving station 1, 4, 24, 35, 42, 48, 57, 60, 68, 73
lighthouse 1, 4, 9, 24, 32, 35, 37, 42, 43, 67
Little Hog Island 76
Lyle gun 59

M

Machipongo 5, 42, 71, 83
Machipongo Creek 48
Machipongo River 81
Magothy Bay 74
Making of Pennsylvania 23
Mangum, Richard and Sherry 3, 61, 63, 64
Marshall, John (Doctor) 27
Matthews, Revell 72

McGeorge, William Jr. 18
Mears, O. F. 19
Metompkin 75
Mockhorn Island 74
Morris, Frederick W. 27
Museum of Northern Arizona 3, 61, 83

N

Narrative About Life on Hog Island, Va. 45
Nassawadox 50
National Geographic 42, 81
Navajo 61
Newhall, Daniel S. 11, 19, 23, 27, 49
Newhall, Thomas 49
New York Herald 34
New York, Philadelphia and Norfolk Railroad (NYP&N) 10, 15, 27, 46, 48, 79, 81
Norfolk Virginian-Pilot 74
Northampton County 7
Northampton County Clerk of Court 69, 83

O

oak pine 37
Old Dominion Gunning and Angling Association 80. *See Revels Island Club*
Old Point Comfort 50
One Woman's West: The Life of Mary-Russell Ferrell Colton 3, 61
Osprey Grove 33
Oyster 8, 72, 76

P

Panic of 1893 66, 67, 70
Parramore family 1
Parramore Island 7, 8, 18, 80, 81
Parramore Land and Improvement Company 9, 18, 23, 69
Parvin, Thomas S. 19, 27
Patterson, C. Stuart 23
Patterson, Grace L. 23
Patton, William A. 27
Pelham School 61
Peninsula Enterprise 53
Pennsylvania and Reading Railroad 67
Pennsylvania Railroad 1, 5, 8, 9, 10, 15, 20, 23, 26, 70, 80
Pennsylvania Railroad Athletic Association 23
Philadelphia Inquirer 68, 69
Philadelphia Ledger 12, 20, 54
Philadelphia School of Design for Women 63
Philadelphia Times 54, 56
Philadelphia, Wilmington, and Baltimore Railroad 50
Phillips, Lizzie 44, 45
Phillips, Ray 44
Phillips, Richard 44, 45
Phillips, Thomas (Captain) 72
photographer 5, 8, 10, 20, 39, 81
Polk, James K. (President) 10
Prouts Island 8
PRR 19, 20, 27, 67
Public Weekly Opinion 67

Q

Quakers (football team) 54, 56
Quinby Inlet 81

R

Rawle, James 27, 68
Real Estate Trust Company 19, 67
Red Bank Landing 42
regatta 82
Reid, Henry 11
Republican Herald 48
Revels Island 80, 81
Revels Island Bay 80
Revels Island Club 80, 81
Richmond Dispatch 68
Robbins House 69
Rum Hill 29, 34, 47

S

San Albano 57, 59, 60
Sandy Island 80
San Francisco Examiner 49
Shiras, George, III 81
Shooting Beach 42
Sims family 28
Sims, John C. 11, 19, 20, 23, 24, 26, 27, 54, 66, 68, 70
Smith, J. E. 60
Smith, Joseph S. 19, 23
Spain 57, 60
Spanish sailors / crew 57, 59, 60
Star-Independent 48
Steam and Steel: The Eastern Shore of Virginia 1870-1884 10, 79
Sterling, Charles 7, 44, 71
Stoner, Samuel 82
Sturgis, John R. (Reverend) 50, 59, 60
Sunshine 6, 48, 50, 51, 52, 53, 68

T

The Hummocks 70
The Nature Conservancy 3, 42, 50
Thomas, George C. 27
Tyler, John (President) 50
Tyrone Daily Herald 24

U

United States Life-Saving Service 60
United States Life-Saving Station 49
University of Pennsylvania 2, 9, 10, 15, 20, 23, 26, 27, 53, 54, 55, 63, 66, 68, 80, 83
University of Pennsylvania Archive Center 23
University of Pennsylvania Athletic Association 23, 54
Upshur, Abel 50
Upshur Bay 81
Upshur, Ben 61
Upshur family 50
Upshur Neck 81
U. S. Coast Guard 74, 75
U.S.S. *Princeton* 50

V

Virginia General Assembly 19
Virginia's Eastern Shore 42

W

Wachapreague 75, 81, 82
Wachapreague Hotel 75
Wallops Beach 75
Wallops Island 73, 75, 80
Wallops Island Association 80
Wallops Island Club 73, 80
Wellman Iron and Steel Company 67
Wellman, Samuel T. 19, 23, 67
Welsh, John Lowher 27, 67
West, Benjamin 82
Whelan, Henry 18
Whitelaw, Ralph T. 42, 70
Wilderness Regained: The Story of the Virginia Barrier Islands 3
Willis Wharf (landing) 8, 42, 48, 51, 53, 66, 72, 76
Willis, Zoro 19
Windsor, William D. 23, 27
Winterthur Museum 12
Woodruff, George Washington 54
Woods Road 35

Y

York Gazette 50

www.ingramcontent.com/pod-product-compliance
Lightning Source LLC
LaVergne TN
LVHW072328100826
845147LV00004B/660

* 9 7 8 1 6 2 8 0 6 4 8 8 9 *